AMERICAN MONOPOLOGY

AMERICAN MONOPOLOGY

A Study of American Business and Monopolies

Jayson Reeves

And
The Hurn Foundation

iUniverse LLC
Bloomington

AMERICAN MONOPOLOGY
A Study of American Business and Monopolies

iUniverse books may be ordered through booksellers or by contacting:

iUniverse LLC
1663 Liberty Drive
Bloomington, IN 47403
www.iuniverse.com
1-800-Authors (1-800-288-4677)

ISBN: 978-1-4917-2491-0 (sc)
ISBN: 978-1-4917-2493-4 (hc)
ISBN: 978-1-4917-2492-7 (e)

Library of Congress Control Number: 2014902838

Printed in the United States of America.

iUniverse rev. date: 02/25/2014

Contents

Introduction

Monopology is a study of monopolies from the American society of people, business, and government. This is the format of how public, private, and government business have worked to establish themselves to the monopoly control of a diversified level of industry markets. Observing the year of 2012 most monopoly and anti-trust legal issues include the discipline of an American society of technology, business, laws, and government. These are legislative and legal issues that must continue to improve with logical enforcement values. Then today's technology such as the internet, some good and bad satellite activity, safer manufacturing, the infrastructure, banking, and various business issues may better apply to the U.S. Constitution and other American social values.

These conditions of important monopoly values are relevant for the equality of most Americans, and then businesses to fairly prosper. Even between the United States Presidencies of Bill Clinton, George Bush, and Barack Obama which includes a few of their cabinet predecessors within various Attorney Generals, they have somewhat ignored certain U.S. Anti-Trust law concerns. These laws are vital within protecting small expandable businesses. Therefore even this being occasionally a local, state, and more so federal government concern these issues can be harmful to the American economy, and the resource of overall businesses if they are not considered properly. Therefore this may include the good, and bad of foreign business related concerns which adds more issues for government to review.

The logic of economic values within laws, and monopolies severely may affect how smaller American businesses expand as they work to prosper with logical growth. This includes the occasional argument that the U.S. Constitution and other U.S. documents like the Declaration of Independence should have been conditionally recognized. Then lately this observation with certain issues of good, and bad foreign relations, or the recent efforts of lawful American business growth could be more sustainable. Considering these factors, all businesses in America have challenges that they must be ready to overcome within these conflicting obstacles. Then understanding this with diversified levels of fairness, American business becomes the logic of how the people better depend on certain corporations, and various business monopolies.

Hundreds of monopolies in America have been established from this resource of business, law, and government with them providing engineering subjects like telephone, water, wastewater, electric, and gas public utility service's as logical business operations, or government operating enterprises. A majority of these firms or corporations are listed on most major stock exchanges to provide investment opportunities, increase their investors or employees wealth, and or to help certain business values of corporate liquidity.

The concept of these public utility monopoly services are providing millions of American homes, farms, businesses, manufacturers, and a vast amount of facilities including government operations with professionally established helpful necessities. Upon these concerns diversified utility services which people pay to have, and maintain are good for health, and safety in all industries, or for the people's duty of just providing and or maintaining comfortable household living standards. This is the understanding which includes most all American social and professional utility resources that are found in hospitals, grocery stores, or even airports, and all other facilities. Therefore these are operational public utilities that people need.

Most corporate business monopolies have patent rights that range from corporate operating disciplines like at Apple Incorporated with the iPod, the iPhone, various computers, and other products. These popular products where part of their former CEO Steve Jobs managing values of technology, and business with Apple Inc. selling an average of 210,000 iPhone's a day between the years of 2010 and 2011. Microsoft Corporation with their inventor, and founder Bill Gates has patent rights to MSDOS, Windows, and various other computer program operating systems. These products like MSDOS and Windows are installed on millions of computers worldwide every year.

Older technology advancements have improved including the patent rights of General Electric Corporation (c/o numerous engineers and designers) with various products. Some of these products consist of light bulbs, electrical transformers, medical equipment, jet engines, locomotive trains, and various other products. This is only part of some business operations in the United States which also appropriate various computer industries with numerous electronic device advancements. Also this includes those advancements of General Electric Corporation observing their diversified business format as a conglomerate.

Other patent rights by Thomas Edison and Alexander Bell have existed for decades besides the harmful abuse that Ameritech Corporation, Enron Corporation, and WorldCom Corporation caused their product, and service disciplines to suffer with throughout the American society financially. This becomes the reason, and concern for the best solutions, and workable components that apply to monopolies. When these and similar monopoly values are established by people, and business resource conditions, the American system of government must be observant. Therefore patents and business can be protected, and productive.

Considering the "Edison, and Bell" Companies established patents, this observation of businesses became a careful process of growth in America. This included certain individuals, and business concerns that are important to all residential, and commercial facility resources that partly affect the economy which consist of various major conditions. These conditional businesses with issues of advanced technology need to be held accountable within complying with U.S. Anti-Trust laws. Observing this, vital prosperity will consist of the highest professional standards of services, contrary to competitive indifferences. Therefore other productive ideas can be offered to the American general public within all people, and or businesses sharing diversified opportunities.

Contrary to these diversified business issues, a vast amount of patent rights and companies are not completely a controlled monopoly, but they do come close enough to control a large part of these "detailed" markets. Their level of market success at these companies may include CEO's similar to Jack Welch formerly of General Electric Corporation or Scott Davis of United Parcel Service Incorporated. These are worldwide operated American corporate businesses whom, are usually well established in their business disciplines of resource. Then their advancements within business expansion come from them being some of the most productive corporate businesses with people that work to be effective with good results. Apple Incorporated, Microsoft Corporation, Kellogg Company, American Telephone & Telegraph Corporation, General Electric Corporation, and various others like some oil companies have been productive corporate businesses in these valued economic resources to society. Also they maintain strong market control, and lawful presence. Then these corporate businesses provide services with various products to the highest industry standards of liability.

The most aggressive monopolies in America with U.S. Anti-Trust law concerns came from companies like American Telephone & Telegraph Corporation (AT&T) with their many subsidiary businesses. Within the many decades following the Great Depression (c/o the 1930s up to the 1980s) the United States government establishing U.S. Anti-Trust laws was part of AT&T, and a few others like General Telephone & Electronics Corporation (GTE) both creating a vast amount of subsidiary businesses. Upon observing the understanding of these massive businesses the U.S. Federal Communication Commission, and the Federal Trade Commission and the has the duty to apply, and enforce appropriate regulation.

During the year 2000 a majority within business control consisted of GTE Corporation whom became Verizon Wireless as the parent company which resulted in them becoming, the largest wireless communication company in the United States. This then included other businesses finding opportunities in America's market of telephone equipment, and services due to the breakup and or restructuring of AT&Ts powerful, and conditionally established monopoly. Therefore besides the business effort of General Telephone & Electronics Corporation it took 60 to 70 years for AT&T and Bell Laboratories to have serious competitors. These business competitors became Verizon, Comcast, Sprint, and at one time some people thought of WorldCom Corporation as a serious competitor.

Another business issue of similarity within the format of an aggressive monopoly was the Standard Oil Company controlling the sale of oil and gas in most American regions. This transition occurred between 1900, to 1920 which years later they changed their name to Amoco Oil Corporation. Before Amoco Oil Corporation, John D Rockefeller with Standard Oil Company went through numerous state and federal court proceedings that changed the way them, and other oil companies do business. This even includes the way Standard Oil Company had distributors that would occasionally sale oil, and gas cheap on the black market side of business during the 1940s. Within the business format of AT&T Corporation, and the Standard Oil Company this was the beginning of the U.S. Anti-Trust law era due to their aggressive control of these markets.

Establishing various U.S. Anti-Trust laws has been somewhat extensive to guide in a good, and completely workable direction, but these laws are vital to improve with consistent enforcement values. Fair competition for hard working people in business is an important equation that helps other businesses prosper with opportunities. Then both AT&T Corporation, and Standard Oil Company (c/o oil, gas, telephone & now internet services) which includes a few other monopolies, and U.S. Anti-Trust law court matters became an important business equation. As these become arguments in the courts vital issues were important as they helped to create U.S. Anti-Trust laws within business equality, and fairness contrary to their vital, and prosperous small and large business operations. Also these business operations offered good conditions of providing changes within improved products, and or services. This therefore then included industry values of an overall management resource of conditions within government regulating business, and their format of extensive liability.

The Amoco Oil Corporation during 1998 was bought out by BP (c/o British Petroleum) which was an economic blow to the American economy, and various safety standards of liability. This is due to the fact that Amoco Oil Corporation was not perfect with certain accidents in America that cost people's lives, and money. Now them becoming BP they have accumulated similar problems throughout their worldwide, and many regional refinery business issues in the United States. This also includes them increasing their market, and revenue share of this global business with their headquarters remaining in the United Kingdom. Understanding this, their value of liability will require an investment with people that have a passion to be good at their job as it applies to "economic disciplines", "safety", and "production".

Observing problems at BP America have also consisted of them not being able to hold certain high standards of liability with business production in the United States. This problem has consisted of the 2010 removal of their CEO Tony Haywood of England, and a new Chief Executive Officer within Bob Dudley whom is an American. BP's Board of Directors approved this transition due to their two major fatal accidents that occurred in Texas City, Texas during 2005, and then during 2010 with their disastrous explosion, and oil leek off the shores of New Orleans, Louisiana. Therefore contrary to their fatal explosions, accidents with contaminated "land and water" issues, this multi-billion dollar (BP) corporate issue has been partly a loss, and issue of liability to America. Then this also means the more liable a large company is, the more control they operate without any, or only a few anti-trust law conflicts.

The concentration of additional problems include BP's main legal, and tax revenue structure which is now applied to Great Britain, and not exclusively the United States with Amoco Oil Corporation. Contrary to other similar corporate businesses, the loss of Amoco Oil Corporation left the United States with a weaker money circulation. This is similar to other American businesses being bought out by foreign businesspeople which also included the quality of work that some Americans make within advancements as professionals. BP's transition with formerly Amoco Oil assets still seems to have an issue of restructuring for the entire business worldwide, therefore some global economic, and liability issues have been observed. This observed factor means that America is far from being left out, but the U.S. has loss government tax revenue from this transaction which includes other major or productive corporate businesses with diversified issues of economic values, financial concerns, and products with good liability.

Understanding the monopoly disciplines of liable management, a vast amount of corporate American businesses have held onto, or have taken control of a percentage of various markets. This is usually part of them providing dependable products, and or services upon which they also attempt to comply with most all laws, and specified product or service standards. The Kellogg Company is a logical example by them holding more than 30% of the market within cereal sales in the United States, and 40% to 70% of cereal sales in most other well developed countries. Kellogg with their CEO John Bryant and these 2011 market sales of one group of their products is what it means to maintain being a productive monopoly, and or managing the control of a large percentage of a market. Therefore this format of business became competitive from various other monopoly driven businesses with some involvement from the American system of government.

A logical definition of "Monopoly" is the liable control of production, and the distribution of products or services by one firm, or a group of firms, and or businesses that are astute within their occupational, or professional values of work. Another defined factor of a "Public Monopoly" consist of those business/government operations like the U.S. Post Office, Amtrak, Tennessee Valley Authority or a local concentration of wastewater, or water treatment business facilities operated, and closely regulated by government. Then a public monopoly such as within a public or government utility providing lawfully effective telephone services, cable television, treated water, and wastewater operations has a duty to ensure the delivery of essential products with valued utility services.

Various production duties of monopoly services are offered to a regional group of citizens based at acceptable prices which are occasionally a disadvantage from some private utility monopoly businesses. The American business monopoly is also characterized by the absence of other similar businesses which conditionally leads to higher or more competitive prices if the lower volume capacity of business survives. Then this becomes a conditional observation as it severely applies to public monopolies owned by the U.S. government like the U.S. Postal Service. Another "U.S. government owned" monopoly value is then observed by Amtrak railroad that is a monopolized passenger train system that has a presence in most all American states to serve its customers. Therefore the format of high prices for services such as comparing small and large electric utilities, transportation, and telecommunication companies also may require the input of competitive improvements observed from their consumers.

During this first decade of 2000 the good, and bad of various monopolies including the United States Postal Service (USPS) have gotten to the point that their absence of competitors is due to the changing times of technology within the U.S. economy. This was subdued by the recent loss in sales of stamps, and other postage rate business concerns causing an absence of customers to the changing times within Internet "E-Mailing", and or "Internet" bill payment services. A format of issues have left their competitors within United Parcel Service (UPS), Federal Express (FedEx), and others making decisions that give them control of maintaining a percentage of these shipping, and delivery business markets. These major market businesses also have a combination of well over a million employees mostly in America, and some internationally. This then means they provide a strong level of support to the American, and global economy.

United Parcel Service Inc. and Federal Express Corp have gained control of shipping markets that are tremendous over the recent decades. The shipping and delivery business in America has become a strong component of government competing with public and private businesses that hold some monopoly values of discipline. UPS with their CEO Scott Davis in 2010 were averaging at least 15.6 million delivery pieces per day worldwide which earned them a total revenue of $49.5 billion dollars. The Federal Express Corporation and their CEO Fredrick Smith also controls a certain amount of this market with revenue of $39.3 billion dollars in 2011. Therefore the United States Postal Service being established in 1775 takes up the other part of millions of letters, and packages per day. This is relevant to them being managed in 2012 by Postmaster General Patrick Donahoe in this extensive market of delivery services throughout the American society, and worldwide.

The objective of good, and more so bad public utility companies, or government owned utilities such as within water, and wastewater treatment plants have become an issue along with the infrastructure in America. These conditions such as within storm water management problems, and faults that are similar to the collapse of levees during 2005 in the City of New Orleans, Louisiana are factual problems within America's infrastructure. Understanding this, the equation of monopolizing utilities with government have enormous issues to correct, even as these "systems are upgraded".

An observation of major engineering, construction, and government work with informative reviews to improve the overall system of water, wastewater, and certain levels of storm water has been vital during the 1st two decades of 2000. This is relevant to more professionals working hard on proper issues. These water and wastewater conditions must be contained in sub-grade pipes for a safe underground flow process. This includes somewhere close to 65%

percent of American cities and some towns that have failed with this concern of mostly obsolete sewers. This has closely been observed in the late 1990s, and the first decade of 2000 by the American Society of Civil Engineers. Then therefore, government and most engineering professionals throughout the American society have their work, and study plans cut out for them without illogical procrastination.

Observing that the August 2005 hurricane Katrina disaster was strong evidence of major problems that exist throughout America's infrastructure, this is the concern for a more workable discipline throughout business, engineering, and government. Understanding the tremendous problem that occurred, all capable Americans (c/o professionalism) must work together to understand what it will take for this infrastructure problem to be corrected. The collapse of these levees is similar to sewers that cave-in throughout American cities, which was also associated with various complacent problems in government that were overlooked. In New Orleans this complacent problem with their former Mayor: Ray Nagan consisted of the cities storm water, wastewater Sewerage and Water Board service monopoly, and the U.S. Army Corps of Engineers whom became part of severe criticism, and various law suits. Actually this disaster of indifference apart from the U.S. Bureau of Reclamation with engineering duties became one of at least 5 of the worst disasters in American history in a 15 year time span.

The Sewerage and Water Board of New Orleans, their "City Engineer", and the U.S. Army Corps of Engineers all have duties to evaluate the need of upgrading various diversified infrastructure, and utility values. This infrastructure issue along with Entergy Corporation is something that should have been considered by most all of Louisiana's state, and federal legislative members of the government including city council members, and any appropriate others. Understanding this obsolete infrastructure issue that failed, the duties of government where not pursued with upgrades by a "productive" monopolized system of business, government, and the best workable standards of engineering. Therefore these business, government, and engineering disciplines where far from their normal need of professionalism, or a high level of liable perfection with workable duties. Then this is understood to be a tremendous civil engineering problem throughout America.

Considering hurricane Katrina this format of American management, economics, financial resources, public health, and technical engineering problems has also led to extensive flooding that cost the American system government too much money. This expensive problem in various regions throughout the United States with supportive concern from the Federal Emergency Management Agency (FEMA) has become a major economic burden to budget values in most parts of the United States. Understanding this, the United States government had to spend hundreds of billions of dollars during the 1st decade of 2000 to correct these damages observing that more problems became a financial overload on most normal citizens.

A weak and obsolete infrastructure becomes a big fault in the American system of government which has affected millions of American businesses, households, vehicles, and the people. This is conflicting especially when FEMA can occasionally loan money (contrary to appropriated grants) to American citizens and businesses when they suffer damages. Then the concept of loans to their businesses sometimes affects consumers with an economy of higher prices that have to be in workable order. Considering this with a bad economy these conflicting issues of grants, lending, and more so borrowing money to correct government and private property damage are a conditional concern. Even as it applies to lending during a bad economy a person, a family (with or without) business, or a operating budget becomes threatened with a loss to some expansion values of personal, small, or large business planning.

Observing the control of various public monopolies operated in a town, city, state, or federal government utility or an infrastructure service capacity, these are business operating values that must be managed professionally. This is a factor observing Commonwealth Edison (c/o ComEd & Exelon) with power plants throughout Chicago, and the United States as separate Edison franchise companies. These Edison companies go along the line of Southern California Edison, Consolidated Edison (New York), Detroit Edison (c/o DTE Energy Co), International Edison, Duke Energy Corporation, and others similar to General Electric Corp being established from an Edison company merger. Also various other electric, and gas utilities such as Northern Indiana Public Service Company (NIPSCO) with Nisource, Arizona Public Service Company (APS), and Pacific Gas & Electric

(PG&E) just to name a few are strong monopolies in their individual regions. These are consolidated regional public utility companies in America that are somewhat diversified geographically as public utility service providing monopolies.

Tennessee Valley Authority (TVA) is a diversified professionally established monopoly upon which these, and other public utility companies are connected through infrastructure specifications, but these connections have different geographic values. TVA uses an enormous amount of transmission towers through the mountains of Tennessee. Then observing places like Chicago, New York, and Detroit (c/o Edison franchises) these companies have more underground transmission electric cables (c/o other sub-grade utilities) that make up their electrical power distribution system.

Most all electric utility routed connections through rural areas with the use of transmission towers all together are considered the American grid for electricity. They are also connected the same way that became evident when Detroit Edison, Consolidated Edison (ConEd) of New York, and certain electric companies equipment failed during the 2003 Northeast American blackout. This blackout affected 55 million people for 3 days in 8 American states. Observing this problem occurred between some southern parts of Canada, and most northeastern states in America it caused well over $5.5 billion dollars in damage.

The American society of public utilities becomes the format of business, and engineering which consist of a vast amount specified equipment with similarities. These are most times monopolies that maintain complete control on their commitment to serve all of their customers geographically whom pay their utility bills. Understanding this, the managing, and continuous maintenance or upgrades of their equipment becomes a vital concern. This means all monopolized utility companies have a distinct duty just like the input, and output of money, and liability that these utility companies generate within business, and government provisions. Then an enormous amount of money is provided as supportive investments in their business operation, and equipment upgrades of responsibility. Therefore considering the first decade of 2000 this compound of infrastructure, and public utility upgrades can have an enormous cost effect in the billions if not more than a trillion dollars.

A vital concern, exist when the people, and government understand the value of dependable American public utility equipment which also requires maintenance with a dependable infrastructure. Public utilities and the American infrastructure are then understood to be compatible government assets. These are American assets that will cost citizens (c/o some government concerns) more (contrary to inflation) if upgrades are not effectively productive. The perfect example is the hundreds or thousands of cars or trucks that have driven into sinkholes, and then these lawsuits hurt local government. These are tragedies that can be mostly be caused by various obsolete sewers, and or occasionally the water companies sub-grade utility equipment.

The population of a town, city, county, or region is part of the basic standard within how much money, and income a public utility monopoly will generate. Their accounting balance sheets within financial, economic and public utility duties apply to their resources of supply, and demand. This is a factor within the utility companies that exist in the smallest rural areas to the largest metropolitan towns, and cities throughout America. Understanding supply, and demand Tennessee Valley Authority has active utilities, and infrastructure values of at least 29 flood control dams, and hydroelectric dams for regional electricity, and flood control. TVA also has a vast amount of coal fired energy plants, natural gas plants, and the combination of turbine combustion plants that supply residential, and commercial electricity with gas for Tennessee, parts of Alabama, Mississippi, and Kentucky.

The conditional business format of utility companies that hold monopoly values are connected to the infrastructure and enter-phase with other public or government utilities. This business structure, usually consist of utility equipment that is positioned, and located throughout their service area in various states. These factors are part of observing certain values that are appropriated by various government regulations. Then the operating format of these utilities, consist of vital regulation. The regulation hear is appropriated from the U.S. Department of Energy, the U.S. Department of Interior, the Bureau of Reclamation, the Army Corps of Engineers, the Energy Regulatory Commission, and other logical state, and federal government agencies. Therefore as other governed agencies like for regulating utilities, and transportation consist of duties in the American system of government, they usually intervene with public, and private sectors of business. Then they all have responsibilities to work together in a resource of planning, and regulated liability.

Besides TVA, and various Edison companies whom maintain progress from patents by Thomas Edison during the 1890s up through today, another variation of monopolies exist within "Railroad Companies" and city "Subway Systems". The concept of a cities bus transit system is somewhat different as it applies to fuel, and some other details, but most of these transit service monopolies started as electric operated systems. This becomes a mix between electric trains, and diesel fuel operated train systems, which applies to the cost of gas, diesel fuel, electricity, and even liquids similar to water.

Understanding diesel or electric railroad transportation the increase of fuel cost has somewhat become similar to utilities which is a vital business, and personnel management issue of responsible concern. Even more the railroad tracks that these rail services operate on are most times part of their monopolized business activity within numerous regions of the United States. This monopolized system of ownership is similar to the market that Amtrak, and others have maintained business progress from in earlier years, and since the 1970s. Also since 1971 Amtrak has been owned, and operated by the United States government under the National Railroad Passenger Corporation with their headquarters located in Washington D.C. at Union Station. Contrary to this factor their established railroad business goes back to the mid 1800's when most trains operated from coal, oil, or wood burning steam engines. Then considering the South Carolina Canal and Railroad Company which operated in the 1830s this has been part of the changing times creating a logical factor of various monopolized business systems of discipline.

Northern Pacific Railroad Company held a large market from 1870 to 1970. They operated on the North America railroad system which included them designing and constructing railroad tracks to provide this service discipline to a vast amount of locations in the United States. In 1956 Northern Pacific Railroad Company was sued by the U.S. Federal government for violations of the Sherman Act due to their control, and ownership of some 40 million acres of land. The conflict was due to their lease agreements and various commodities. Then now, the U.S. government who helped them buy the land and receive the land, conditionally wanted to regain a logical amount of control of the land along with other people having business concerns.

During 1970 Northern Pacific Railroad formed an agreement with other railroad companies to become Burlington Northern Railroad which became Burlington Northern & Santa Fe (c/o BNSF) which increased their market share. One of the major shareholder's, consist of Warren Buffet with Berkshire Hathaway. Considering this array of diversified railroad systems their continued economic and financial restructuring became important. This was factual due to their enormous resource of business that lacked some controlled values throughout the many regions of the United States with a variation of railroad companies having endured a conditional value of mostly good, and some bad economic, and operating disciplines.

The concept of diesel fuel has been relevant to one conditional resource of railroad transportation, but numerous electric train railroad systems became advanced with Amtrak, and most subway systems throughout most all major cities. Amtrak passenger trains have a monopoly on long distance railroad travel for a vast amount of Americans. Contrary to the transportation issues of Amtrak, tens of millions of Americans take a subway train every day from one part of a city to another. This American system is advanced with electric train routes which include a ticket pricing system that is managed from consumer payments, and reviewed by managing "Local Transit" authorities annually. The government and business nature of this exist so that it is fair to all citizens that depend on these services. Therefore considering this format of a monopoly, a vast amount of large cities with subway systems consist of a governed money circulation. Then this issue of good, and occasionally bad revenue values include budget issues within overall business. These economic and budget values just like other monopolies must be astute with their duties of governed managing.

Another money circulation issue where U.S. Anti-Trust laws have been waved is the conflicting expansion of the largest banking institutions in America. The mortgage and debt crisis from 2007 moving thru 2011 has shifted losing banks to be bought out by larger banks which are controlling more money than most times in American history. Considering this crisis the small or mid-size banks made bad loans, and put themselves out of business apart from U.S. Anti-Trust law conflicts. Concerning this, the American banking industry which made some progress and some failures with conflicting issues of stability will hopefully improve in the near coming future. This consideration of facts will be determined if the U.S. economy improves with the people being able to pay off loans, and other obligations.

Observing the American market for mortgages becoming a business within a banking monopoly capacity, this only may exist in an extremely small town or by companies such as Century 21 Realtors, and Coldwell Banker. As it applies to the United States the competitive mortgage market is worth over $12 trillion dollars (c/o 2009) with banking institutions that have been observed as too large to fail, and in some cases too large to even manage. Considering this since the repeal of the Glass Steagall Act, the American society has had to be concerned about issues like leveraging properties to sale.

As strong companies like Century 21 Real Estate and Coldwell Banker Real Estate LLC have monopolized, certain markets with a concentration of banking conflicts have become even more complex than ever. This is factual observing the activity within large expanding commercial banks, and investment banks, but very few bankers renovate commercial and residential facilities and cut grass to sale the properties that they temporally control. Observing this the real estate issues at Century 21 Realtors, and Coldwell Banker have been overloaded with properties that don't sale fast enough. Then contrary to realtors as the banks have control of too much money without truly maintaining productive management outside of bank business disciplines of formal responsibility, the American economy, and people suffered.

Even observing small town banks, and certain new U.S. Anti-Trust law concerns small investors lose, and bank customers are stalled with various difficulties. This is becoming part of the anger of middle class Americans trying to move ahead. Contrary to prosperity they are suffering from bad regulation, and too big to fail bullies, or corporations rated as Junk Bond issues in the financial markets. Therefore how the U.S. Constitutional Power of the "Highest Courts" becomes vital with these issues, and various decisions for the future is an awareness of laws, and active business.

CHAPTER ONE

History Of American Monopolies

An American Study Of Business & Monopolies

History Of American Monopolies

Our history of the American system of monopolies with business, and government goes back centuries. These industry, and competitive business values where established with a variation of products like petroleum, coal, railroads, boats, roadways, bridges, dams, clothing's, food, guns, cars, telegraphs, houses, then telephones, mail delivery, and other valued business concerns. Also from the 1800s to 2012 a vast amount of monopolies and businesses dealing with subjects like treated water, wastewater, gas, and electric or mechanical products, and services have become regional monopolies that people depend on having. This has become a massive resource of Americans conducting business as monopolies along with various dependable public utility businesses with "utility holding company act" responsibilities.

Since the early 1900s most all public utility companies are still working to make their monopolized markets a vital level of appreciation, and liability. Understanding this, the American infrastructure was created, and it has been changing for centuries. These changes, includes how the infrastructure has been incorporated with all public utility operating equipment, but cost effective maintenance cannot be overlooked. This has been valuable in America from the Presidential days of Abraham Lincoln to now with President Barack Obama when the infrastructure is recognized along with other utilization necessities.

Another resource of liability that improves products, services, and the infrastructure includes the governed involvement, and activities of the American system of local, county, state and federal government regulators. Besides a population of hundreds of millions of American citizens, and numerous corporate businesses all local, state, and federal government officials with agencies observes, and regulates millions of products, and services annually. This also includes the provisions and enforced regulatory concern for the people, land, air, and water (c/o the Environmental Protection Agency) in most all logical regions of America. Therefore after centuries of product, and service developments the existence of the U.S. Constitution with amendments also became a factor with safety, and U.S. Anti-Trust laws. These are the laws that provided regulation for logical and fair opportunities to businesses being regulated from the 1930s up to the present 2000 millennium time of today.

The changing times (c/o good and bad issues) of controlled markets besides live stock (c/o horses, chickens, hogs, and cattle) which includes other products, and services are a diversion of indifference from public utility monopolies. These are livestock products that along with various commodities have become valuable to industry, and the people of the United States. As horses (c/o buggies) use to be a common form of transportation, various public and private businesses were established, and then they were closely regulated by local, state, and the U.S. federal government. This became the observation of various monopolized business systems in America as patents were documented through government, and even conferred by investors. Therefore the creator of an invention has a right by law of government for a vast amount of product ownership disciplines of making, using, and the sale of patent rights over a period of time.

Throughout the 1800s up to the recent times of 2000 a vast amount of factors within people, and even the blacksmith metal working process had various production values. As years went on this increased with the demand for steel made structured products like guns, boats, cars, trucks, electrical transformers, bridges, airplanes, and other items. The format of structural steel construction items, and product system components made in various steel mills of a corporate capacity expanded by satisfying public utility and lawful product equipment requirements. Then this provided products like boats, cars, trucks, bridges, and railroad trains with tracks to be valuable products, by-products, and various standardized industry components. This is the format of American industry that has become important to the American people, and their need for products to be reliable, and dependable.

Boat travel in America and throughout the world started before the 1800s, but they made advancements in various ways which occurred with increasing conditions of technology. Between England, and America the invention of steam powered engine boats, and trains during the 1830s and 1850s continued to make advancements. Other transportation resources included the development, and process of building U.S. Naval ships, ocean cruse-ships for passengers or cargo, submarines for defense, civilian watercrafts, and various boating industry product concerns. These ships have been around for centuries, but the most modern ships lately have been designed, and built by companies like General Dynamics, and Northrop Grumman shipbuilding. Considering today these ships have become well advanced with nuclear energy operating technology upon which these companies, certain colleges, universities, and government have made advancements from research and development.

Over the decades from the 1970s shipping harbors have become innovated for import and export business markets. This is the concern that out of the hundreds of shipping ports in America the largest and most productive ports are in Louisiana, Texas, California, and West Virginia. These diversified port authorities throughout the American society consist of cruse-ships, fishing vassals, local and or national commodities of food. Then this includes oil and coal with some international goods, other deliveries, and marinas of local boating value, and overall waterway infrastructure resources.

There are smaller shipping, and boat manufactures that specialized in a diversified industry for people with concerns of traveling, or working within professions, and occupations on America's diversified waterways. Understanding this they therefore have a variation of the watercraft products for the American general public, and business values to satisfy various consumers. The fishing industry has come a long way similar to boats, and even submarines that are used for defense, research, and even the oil industry of offshore oil exploration, drilling, and distribution. Observing this concept of the boating, and shipping product industries, America with other countries have made business, and boat travel a severely relevant factor for a variety of product, and service demands.

The level of advancements can be recognized in the American automobile industry with diversified vehicles for everyday people, and industry. When Henry Ford (c/o Ford Motor Co) was starting the manufacturing process of cars in the 1920s with rivals General Motors Corp, and Chrysler Corp whom were following this creation of a large market, there was not as a single monopoly easily established. This industry concern expanded competitively to the extent of how between 2006 and 2012 Alan Mulally the recent CEO of Ford Motor Company kept this company as an automaker productive through a bad American economy. Therefore this large market of high cost ticket items consist of engineers, lawyers, and other professionals observing government regulation for massive manufacturing, and industry standards. These are issues that had to be evaluated with the American economy.

Locomotive railroad travel during the 1880s became a strong industry concern which today (c/o 2010) consist of more diversified freight, and passenger train services. Understanding these diversified railroad services this industry continued to become innovated with various expanding liability disciplines, and business controlled markets. These were market and industries such as the distribution of coal and even live stoke like chickens and cows. Therefore the distribution was created to be astute.

Some railroads since the 1930s have managed to become the subway system of today in most largely populated cities. Observing these subway train systems one of the more detailed factors is that most of these subway trains are electric operated, and then there is an electric utility bill or agreement to the transit authority. Also another factor includes a diversified condition of labor union, and nonunion work force of employees with duties that must be managed on a large, and or logical scale. Considering this factor local and long distance travel became detailed.

Subway train systems in places like Chicago, New York City, Washington D.C., Los Angeles, and a few others earn logical revenue every day. These cities usually have millions of riders a day on these subway train systems. Then these trains and railroad systems require maintenance, upkeep, and upgraded rail system components. Therefore even with electricity to move trains, the people in business whom worked on these active systems of moving passengers, and various capacities of freight have had conditional arguments, conflicts, and labor or business agreements as they earned income. As constructive arguments occurred, this has help improve various engineering, safety, and economic laws with workable business values.

The New York City Subway system is owned by the City of New York, and leased to the New York Transit Authority which is a subsidiary agent of the Metropolitan Transportation Authority consisting of 468 train stations in 2012. This subway system today as of being the 7th largest in the world has operated for over 100 years. Contrary to these factors during the first decade of 2000 on occasions this subway system has been the target of terrorist plots where security had to be increased by the New York City Transit police, and other law enforcement authorities. This was considered after the September 11, 2001 attacks, and a 2005 subway bombing in Loudon, England.

The Chicago subway system is the second largest American system behind New York, and it is called "the L" which is due to its (EL) elevated track design which operates above various downtown roadways. Chicago's subway system is managed by the Chicago Transit Authority whom also manages the city's bus transportation system. This Midwest Illinois regional electric train system also has a Metropolitan (the Metro) train for Chicago suburbs, and the South Shore (c/o NICTD) system as the Northwest Indiana Commuter Transportation District which comes together as 1 major hub in downtown Chicago. Other subway systems that are active consist of Washington D.C., Los Angeles, and the San Francisco system which connects to some parts of Oakland, California.

Everyone that was employed on various projects like constructing railroad track systems had consistent or continuous work for various people over the last two centuries. Then many decades ago there was those people that barely earned a wage like some "sharecroppers, or prison inmates" upon which includes labor and non-labor workers whom stayed conditionally busy. These people constantly working on infrastructures like railroad tracks which sometimes included bridges, roads, and utilities became vital. Then these components where observed for their diversified travel resources which has appropriately helped numerous transportation routes in America.

Managing railroads from the 1880s up until the 2000s has consisted of diversified investments, and the design of specified tracks for specified trains. These business and technical engineering values with the U.S. government are issues that are part of why the U.S. Railroad Act of 1862 was established. This was the monopolized control of government work from U.S. President Abraham Lincoln, and the United States Congress. Observing these separated powers of government, they made this decision to help build an infrastructure system of railroad tracks, and telegraph utility lines.

Over the decades it's been understood that public and private business monopolies also depend on various other public utilities. These factors of the American system of monopolies, and government have been responsible to grasp most of these markets with regulatory discipline. This also consist of the understanding that they somewhat provide taxable revenue, but as public utilities make advancements "the American infrastructure" has been held to some delays. These issues make this a slow and detailed effort in some regions along with the process for vital upgrades that still become an issue. Understanding this concern a vast amount of American city officials forgot how important it is for the city government, and public utility monopolies are to become and maintain a workable resource together.

Considering various facts the city of Detroit filed for bankruptcy during July of 2013. This was a problem which like some other cities consisted of infrastructure, housing, and school closing problems with various crimes. These conflicts lead to law suits, and a dysfunctional city that could have been managed better. Then occasionally (c/o Detroit, Mi. and some other major cities) this becomes a logical, and diversified process of maintaining an upgraded infrastructure when "government assets must be fixed" with a combination of workable components.

Contrary to the good and bad economic times of Detroit with that automobile industry, Detroit's monopolized electric utility is DTE Energy which used to be named Detroit Edison. Part of the overall restructuring as it applies to the City of Detroit, utilities, and schools is part of the loss in population. In 1970 Detroit had 1.5 million people, and as of 2010 they have 713,777 people which is a loss of more than 50% of the population. Understanding this, a vast amount of issues has changed even as in 2013 they have been critically observed for having 78,000 abandon properties.

Observing other markets, and components of a monopoly this included the years during the 1830s, and 1840s of developing telegraphs with Morse code. The "Telegraph and Mores code" was developed by Samuel Morse, and then soon after came telephones by Alexander Bell. Samuel Morse also received one of the first telephone and utility pole contracts throughout the United States starting at $30,000.00 in the 1840s to manage the design, and construction of these monopolized utility structures. Decades later we now have cell phones with towers, and the internet which have created various market monopolies with strong percentages of sales, and professional disciplines. Then this becomes the work to hold customer satisfaction in this new and arbitrary market astute with liable dependability.

The telegraph by way of Morse code and the Western Union Company contrary to their business existence today became a monopoly for Americans, and some other developing countries. This became the technological process of sending telegrams to other people, businesses, and government in far-away places at a good rate of speed. These advancements throughout business, and industry from scientist, inventors, engineers, then computer programmers, and others is part of what makes America, and some other well developed countries maintain a society of resourceful progress.

The arbitrary industry concerns of the internet and cell phones are part of a new infrastructure within wired and now wireless communication, which includes an increasing use of cell phone towers with commercial satellites. The format of commercial satellite use, have been lately lacking appropriate, and vital regulation from regional entities of the American system of state and federal government duties. These Separation of Power issues in government is part of factual disciplines that the U.S. Constitution was written, and established over 235 years ago, but today it still applies to amended old, and new laws with regulatory disciplines. Then the regulation of various products and services are part of the domestic tranquility, and prosperity for justifiable living.

The executive, legislative, and judicial duties of power with government become vitally important to the enforcement, and creation of established laws. These laws and the equation of separated government power are outlined with U.S. Anti-Trust legal values, and Amendments to the U.S. Constitution to improve the American society which includes business equality. All branches of the American system of government recognize this equation of small, large, or monopolized businesses which goes along the lines of some other social concerns like the economy.

With various strong market components most telephones, and communication business issues became effective for most all American regions, but U.S. Anti-Trust laws in the factor of "trust busting" have been a harmful problem. These became conflicting and destructive issues of hurt and timeless ridicule to some American small business owners from expanding. Then these levels of fair and unfairly considered business within American values are conflicting as it applies to small expanding business owners, and even investors that must protect or observe the invested interest of their business. Therefore it becomes inevitable that laws are enforced without costing businesses too much of their reliable income.

Understanding certain law values of the U.S. Constitution which more people including various professionals today slightly try to ignore has been a problem for business, and various socially productive resources in America. These issues of older technology were part of state and federal Constitutionally Amended laws which became the regulatory base of importance. This format of laws also became part of a telecommunication industry that has gained logical control of certain markets with research, and extensive levels of business, and product expansion. Contrary to this control of products, and services over the decades various markets have changed. Some of these markets include how the American Oil industry has made a vast amount of changes in technological advancements, and their observation to comply with a variation of U.S. Environmental Protection Agency regulatory laws, and most U.S. Anti-Trust laws. These historical laws have been part of the changing times of American industry.

A certain level of industry changes occurred during the business ownership, and tenure of John D Rockefeller which included their aggressive business activities at Standard Oil Company during 1900 to 1911. Then the concept of U.S. Anti-Trust laws were argued during 1911 at the U.S. Supreme Court level, but leading up to the recent times (c/o 2000), environmental regulation, and safety have become vital. This became the obstruction of additional cost concerns that were compared with too big to fail business issues. These were businesses like British Petroleum (BP) with their CEO's Tony Haywood, and then Bob Dudley which seem too be a business that was too big, and or complex to manage. After BP's buyout transaction of the 100 plus year old American business concern of "Amoco Oil formerly known as Standard Oil" this company seem too complex to manage with U.S. founded Anti-Trust laws. This became a business issue in the American oil industry as a corporate giant that consisted of productivity that also had too many fatal accidents.

Understanding high levels of efficiency being part of the economic problems of the United States too many companies like some banks in America have seem to become too big to manage as they are considered too big to fail as well. Then this also seems to be an

9

issue of being too big for some people, and executives to coordinate these diversified industry issues that must be managed properly. This becomes vitally important within their common business values of survival. Therefore it must be observed as important that we review or argue the 235 plus year document called the United States Constitution for a better equation of opportunities, and responsibilities.

Managing American oil companies with their U.S. domestic, and international business markets upon which they work towards management, and labor values within exploring, and or producing oil, and gas from worldwide resources has accumulated various problems. These technical problems have somewhat been a loss to certain vital industry disciplines as it applies to the environment, and safety on or off various job sites. This was the losing factor of BP during the tenure of Tony Haywood whom was in command during the Texas City, Texas fatal explosion, and the Gulf of Mexico BP explosion, and oil leek disaster.

As certain international issues of transition from the American oil industry has consisted of environmental conflicts, some alarming terrorist concerns have been a threat to some oil workers. These more so foreign conflicts of various issues for Americans working in various other international regions had been potentially threatened by war time conditions. Contrary to a vast amount of American technology having helped the Middle East drill and produce oil reserves these regions still became dangerous to anyone. This is where the U.S. government and major industrial businesses try to work together on coordinated issues of national security, and safety.

Some other valuable disciplines of managing large industrial businesses include other oil companies, and how they maintain safety, and stable financial liquidity. This was a factor of forcing some oil companies to merge from being two corporate businesses, and then becoming one. ExxonMobil Corporation, ConocoPhillips, and even United Continental Holdings airline as it applies to the U.S. airline transportation industry are logical examples of combined business industry mergers. These are issues that they occasionally have to argue in the courts which have made some industry standards safer and livable to employees, citizens, investors, government and other businesses.

Understanding oil drilling, and production in the early 1900s to the 1940s American oil companies primarily drilled in the United States. This occurred up until their enter-phase with global oil resources, and national economies between European countries, North Africa, and more so the Middle East. Some of the conflicts include the oil embargo crisis during the early 1970s upon which a Middle Eastern war temporarily disrupted America's oil supplies from Middle Eastern countries. These have been long term issues from Middle Eastern countries which during the Richard Nixon U.S. Presidency the Arab, and Israeli war had many international conflicts of stopping U.S. oil supplies.

Observing international and U.S. domestic concerns has been part of businesses within various industries that tried to expand with good and bad resources of the American economy. From the U.S. Presidential activities of John F. Kennedy, Lyndon Johnson, and Richard Nixon the Vietnam War was also a critical part of the American economy. As the changing times of government, and business occurred a worldwide banking conflict of business has recently created an economic crisis similar to the 1970s that includes an American debt crisis. This crisis along with banking in the United States vitally consisted of the increasing cost of gas, and oil being a foreign, and U.S. domestic issue with certain conflicts. A factual observation, also consist of how American oil companies have had to stop work due to violent conflicts in these international oil producing regions. Then throughout America the people now have had to constantly readjust to various cost and social issues in this reoccurring conflict of industry, and economic matters.

American business being somewhat different from most concerns of monopolies operating in America is observed mostly with the public utility sectors of business. They started expanding in the late 1870s with Thomas Edison, Alexander Bell, George Eastman, and others. Understanding this, a vast amount of electric, gas, communication, and water resource utility companies monopolized, and expanded. Therefore with this enormous amount of technology, the American format of research has helped establish public utilities with most times good obligated commitments of service.

Considering the 1990s these innovated businesspeople, were different from the former Enron Corporation with their CEO Ken

Lay, and WorldCom Corporation with their CEO Bernard Ebbers. This became factual as both Kenneth Lay, Barnard Ebbers, and a few other high level corporate executives misguided, and manipulated the integrity of innovated business in America. Observing this, there are still people that are inclined to conditions of greed that refuse to make the most logical or honest efforts in business.

Observing these and various other business or government public utility monopolies some conditions of wastewater treatment facilities started to become more active in most local cities with political, professional, and government involvement. Political conflicts are potentially part of the worse factor for these utilities operated, and regulated by government when the leadership applies to much disregard for professionalism. Some sad political factors consist of the need of engineering professionals, and "Not Too Many Lawyers" trying to do Government Engineering Work at wastewater treatment plants which applies to City Engineering Department disciplines. The city government of Gary, Indiana has done this worse than a vast amount of other cities, and towns during the 1990s.

The good, and bad of American professional and government engineers which applies to wastewater, and more so storm water infrastructure systems has engaged in various low or high level professional conflicts. These are conflicts were knowledge, and experienced people are occasionally not active in vital engineering projects. This includes certain occupational and professional levels of work done properly, and or productively. Then those people that have no experience or ambition in the field of professional engineering with design skills, knowledge of specified equipment, and the use of materials become a problem of severe corrections. This has been relevant with the American society, and others whom cannot afford or don't apply professional standards that become expensive conflicting mistakes, and or damages. A factual observation includes the "Hurricane Katrina flooding" disaster that destroyed American people, and property from New Orleans to places as far away as Iowa, and northern Indiana.

Over the decades in America there are small and large monopolies that experienced extensive growth with city population increases, and or government regulation. The city of Chicago after the major fire of 1871 made that city and region somewhat a perfect resource for new and advanced utilities. This was the beginning of the Chicago electric utility monopoly of the Isolated Lighting Company that was a valuable business operation in 1881. Then they became the Western Electric Light Company which was also an agent of the Edison Companies throughout the city of Chicago. In 1907 the Chicago Commonwealth Edison Company started becoming a well-developed electric utility monopoly serving one of the largest markets in America. The public utility of Commonwealth Edison (ComEd) today (c/o 2010) is still the controlling or resourceful monopoly that provides Chicago, the suburban areas, and North Eastern Illinois with electrical power distribution services.

The late 1800s and early 1900s became a time when public utilities such as Commonwealth Edison, Consolidated Edison, Detroit Edison, Tennessee Valley Authority, American Electric Power, and others began producing electricity at high rates. As time went on the conversion from windmills to the constructing of coal fired energy plants became unit operations that help provide electricity for most all logical indoor and outdoor places throughout America. This became the condition of establishing, and pursuing studies of engineering for electrical, mechanical, and gas feasibilities throughout the American society. These utility issues could be applied to every roadway, residential, and commercial facility when appropriate. By the 1950s every school, hospital, home, church, government facility, and other places substantially like manufacturing businesses were able to operate with utility access or could be accessible with most all public utilities.

In northern Indiana with a vast amount of steel mills (contrary to other industries) using high rates of gas, and electricity a major utility monopoly operation became the Northern Indiana Public Service Company (NIPSCO) which has operated for a century. This monopolized business reorganized with them taking on a parent company within Nisource which occurred in the late 1990s. During the first decade of 2000 this was one of the major public utility corporate mergers that was pursued carefully. Then numerous others seem to follow with similar transactions.

Observing small and or large electric, and or gas utility companies these issues became active in various stock ownership transactions. Also lately some utility companies have been part of some of the most critical mergers in our recent times. They also are different in the sense that they rarely changed their corporate monopoly name. This was important and relevant to keep their residential and commercial base of utility customers logical with lawful information, and services. Therefore the major issues of a business monopoly with concerns of liability have discipline not to lose their customer resource of trust, and the value of working to provide customers with various services.

Today various periods of expansion occurs when companies and markets bring interesting, and workable products to the American people. This has been similar to Apple Incorporated and Microsoft Corporation during 1990 to 2010, but the infrastructure has different work that includes more professionals and government officials that must get it right. Understanding the adjustments in the infrastructure, and more so the history of developing the first computer, this consisted of various electronic products, and the UNIVAC computer system.

The logical product development of the UNIVAC started in the 1940s which was a very large and heavy computer system that took up a large portion of a room for small or conditional amounts of data to be processed. This computer used vacuum tubes, and large magnetic disk. Then a more advanced system used keypunch cards instead of microchips, or hard drives which help the programming and hardware operating systems with various data being processed. Fiber optic utility lines were included, and then the storing or installing of data became an issue of diversity. This process became compatible to a vast amount of computers with a memory base, and the operating system procedures that made them follow certain electronic programmed commands. Therefore this became part of the information technology (IT) base of activity with data being processed, and transitioned between most people in various American, and worldwide locations.

Observing the technology of a computer storing memory, and processing data on a hard drive became effective with products from businesses like Seagate Technology, and their founder Alan Shugart. The valuable work of Alan Shugart as an engineer whom established Seagate Technology during the late 1970s was partly a stable monopoly with the computer hard drive. Seagate Technology became a hard drive manufacturing business with very few competitors that created a productive market of hundreds of millions of hard drives sold in 30 years. Seagate Technology's present CEO being Stephen Luczo has been involved in this company earning billions of dollars in revenue during 2009, and 2010. From there in the 1960s up to the 1980s, and 1990s computers continued to have major changes as they became smaller, and faster with advanced hard drives, microchips, and microprocessors.

The computer monitor went from a two color monochrome screen in the 1960s and 1970s to the video graphic array (VGA) carded screen which gave the operator an array, or a multitude of different colors to use. This became the process of graphics, design with computer aided drafting (CAD) that is part of an enormous market for education, personal computer use, and a large variety of Architecture & Engineering use in professional business offices. Theoretically the VGA system became pitcher perfect as of the mid 1990's. Other corporations became more involved which consisted of International Business Machines (IBM), Digital Equipment, and later Apple Inc. with the Macintosh computer. From there an enormous amount of electronic products included other businesses making the effort to become advanced with computer science issues of this format of technology.

As the hardware, and software of computers made advancements this expanded into internet services that incorporated wireless telephones with internet computer service capabilities. This then connected people, businesses, and government that somewhat eliminated and or restructured the operating use of hundreds of thousands of public payphones nationwide. The changing format of technology consisted of a majority of people using cell phones with computer applications of software programs. Also this changed the American infrastructure with advancements that eliminated products, and services like with public payphones. Then other technology replacements consisted of vacuum tubes being eliminated from computers, monitors, radios, and televisions. These are the technology adjustments that where applied to televisions becoming the flat screen (invention) with internet capability systems. This also included VGA capabilities, which is similar to high definition (HD) cable T.V. systems. Then other products like microchips and VGA screens with fiber technology have been used in the recent 1990, and 2000 decades with large rates of production.

The UNIVAC was sought by many corporations during its research and development at the University of Pennsylvania. This is similar to the process of the invention of the "Television" which became a product in the majority of households throughout the United States over time. American companies and government that found interest in the UNIVAC product consisted of Northrop Aviation, the U.S. Bureau of Census, the U.S. Department of Defense, and Sperry Corporation. From there the concept of computers with wired and wireless connections became part of the internet and other means of electronic networking. Similar to telephones a vast amount of people were able to network with other people far apart from each other like in other American states, and or other countries. Therefore the external hardware process of the computer was one of a few levels of advancement with some patent law concerns which especially included the internal software operating system of computers becoming another resource of advancements.

Bill Gates establishing Microsoft Inc. patented one of the first disk operating systems (DOS) that manages most computer programmed files, memory, and data to create a productive computer operating system of components. This product expansion with MSDOS and then Windows software with various other monopolized computer software products became superior to most all computer operating disciplines. Also most computers became user friendly with more people becoming productive with the use of computers. These are products that offered IBM compatible computer equipment, and their system operating procedures for internal data user friendly activity on more than 70% of all computers developed in America.

Contrary to Microsoft Corp (c/o IBM compatibility systems) the only other software conflict or competitor was that of Apple Incorporated Macintosh computer language. Understanding this level of advanced technology, these two computer operating systems were different, but for everyone using a computer it was clear that the operating details like a keyboard for typing, and the "off, and on" switch were normal. Then other vital products became part of standard connections such as printers, copiers, fax machines, and even screen projectors. Considering these products with various details this provided an interest and atmosphere with more young people, and various older people becoming computer literate at growing rates.

As American business monopolies moved into the early 1900s up to the 1970s, and today telephone communication cables were installed throughout the United States, and this upgraded the American telecommunication infrastructure. These levels of advancement occurred in most common places in America, and various parts of the world. Western Electric Company, Inc was a subsidiary of AT&T that monopolized a business system for telephone equipment, and services.

Besides the electrical engineering work from George Shawk of Western Electric, this company included inventor Elisha Gray in the early 1900s. As Elisha Gray created a majority purchase of Western Electric Manufacturing Company his commitments were recognized as valuable. Then over time other companies such as Graybar was established in his behalf as these advancements provided business monopoly disciplines. Then these "internal and external telephone equipment" levels of prosperity became valuable throughout America, and in some worldwide markets.

These business issues of Western Electric existed between the states of Ohio, Illinois, and then New York City becoming their new headquarters. Besides their active business in Chicago and Cleveland the Western Electric Company has operated at least 11 factories from 1904 to 2000 in various different states. Considering millions of dollars earned including some U.S. defense contract work with more people employed in this manufacturing, and service industry, the existence of this monopoly survived through a vast amount of good, and bad times in America. Also these became some of the braking points for the partnership of Enos Barton, and Elisha Gray with the Western Electric Company, and the Graybar Company which is headquartered in St. Louis, Missouri.

The combination of these two men within Enos Barton, and Elisha Gray establishing Western Electric Company with others consist of them working close with business relations to Western Union, and American Telephone & Telegraph. This effort within business became an exceptional equipment manufacturing monopoly for telephones, and most all telephone connection equipment with services. Establishing this level of manufacturing and service resources of working together created certain business, and technology based products which provided customer contract agreements all over the United States. Understanding these business values of 1915 the Western Electric Company was distinctively becoming a manufacturing, and service unit that monopolized certain telecommunication business issues with American Telephone & Telegraph. These two companies created patented products that existed for most all residential, and commercial telephone equipment, and general service agreements.

Throughout this business monopoly process with AT&T and the Western Electric Company these values of a monopoly started to expand. This expansion was prosperous with millions of dollars earned, and invested from various telecommunication service issues, and equipment. These companies within AT&T's product, and services with Western Electric Company provided a residential and commercial concept of agreements for all telephones to customers, and the AT&T connections to most all facilities.

AT&T's only rival during a considerable amount of time has been GTE Corporation which stood for General Telephone & Electronics Corporation. Western Electric and AT&T held strict guild lines on all consumer telephones which was outlined that No Non-AT&T/ Western Electric telephone equipment be connected to AT&T's internal and external cable line connections. The customer would own the telephone on their premises, but AT&T had an army of employees that would conduct inspections to make sure no unauthorized brand of telephone was being used with the AT&T service agreements.

Observing all monopolized public utilities which telephone company issues apply occasionally consisted of values from the U.S. Congress with legislative concern in 1935. This was the format of establishing the Public Utility Holding Company Act that has various law functions. One of its functions was to keep regulated utility or monopolized businesses from engaging in unregulated business activities. This was due, too the factual resource and discipline that public utility companies were occasionally complex to regulate. Therefore with an enormous amount of investors it became law that these public utility monopolies had to obtain approval from the Securities and Exchange Commission. These are issues of when large financial transactions may occur before certain businesses are engaging in non-utility or closely regulated business activities that where important to be kept separate, and or sometimes within an individual state's law jurisdiction.

The concept of non-utility and public utility corporate or government owned monopolies were business issues to keep separate as it applies to an electric utility company that sells or operates streetcars, or the subway trains sold to a transit system authority. Then various cost, may apply to the operational resources of electricity similar to treated water. These are business issues that must be conducted without the utility company trying to control the train service business or vice-versa as nether business, or a monopoly should control the other. Observing this concept of U.S. Anti-Trust law values more security could be achieved from more businesses other than one trying to control too many other regulated businesses. Then each level of historical or patented monopoly business values becomes a format of how the American society is valued in business from the changing times.

CHAPTER TWO

The United States Anti-Trust Law Era

An American Study Of Business & Monopolies

The United States Anti-Trust Law Era

Understanding the 19th and 20th century (c/o now the 1st decade of 2000) era of U.S. Anti-Trust law conditions in America can be consolidated into various factors of timing, and industry conflicts. The intervention of state and federal government court proceedings and legislature is valid within how anti-trust laws are partly created, and enforced. These are resourceful government procedures that are part of logical business opposition that observes unfair levels of commodity, and or product or service control between various businesses.

The format of monopolized business issues of industry mostly exist at some small, and more so various large corporate levels of business that understand, and keep up with this legal condition of awareness. Contrary to this fact small productive businesses must take observation on these anti-competitive business issues as they manage survival business details, or the tools of various trades. Therefore the U.S. Anti-Trust law era has consisted of the times during the transitioning expansion of businesses. These are businesses that grew in a controlling, and or aggressive capacity with various products, and services that people pay for to have, and or need.

A major observation of these U.S., and occasionally worldwide anti-trust concerns of industry within markets have consisted of the most common necessities of products, and services. These residential, commercial, and even mobile items or services are appropriate with economic and professional support for customers. This is based on a factual anti-trust sector of markets that consist of various services with expensive products. These establishments consist of the electrical power and natural gas distribution industry, the wired and wireless telephone industry, the oil and liquefied gas industry, the diversified shipping industry, and a variation of transportation industries with appropriate markets. Then today this also includes the computer software industry, and some other programming applications with product related issues.

Before BP's buyout purchase of Amoco Oil Corporation one of Americas most active, and aggressive companies within U.S. Anti-Trust law sectors of business was the correlation of Standard Oil Company. This becomes the understanding that Amoco Oil

Corporation was one of many "brake-up" predecessors of the Standard Oil Company. Following these activities with good, and more so bad management, and government values to observe anti-trust law activities in the American society is an issue that fell into an economic and social tailspin. These conflicting times are similar to the 1920s economic depression that affected a vast amount of product manufacturing. This oil business monopoly established by John Rockefeller in 1863 became the sole provider of oil, and gas throughout two-thirds of the United States up until 1906.

Years following 1906, the Standard Oil Company and John Rockefeller's business assets, and liquidity began expanding into uncomfortable public and business opinions of controlling a market. This became crucial within times before a critical restructuring of the entire company. Apart from them being one of richest and most powerful companies in the world the U.S. Supreme Court ruled, and ordered the company in 1911 to dissolve its combination of companies under the Sherman Antitrust Act. Therefore massive and careful changes had to be made.

Years after the United States vs. the Standard Oil Company was rendered relevant to U.S. Anti-Trust law arguments, severe violations observed by the U.S. Supreme Court's decision became critical to other business issues. One factor about this legal case is that Standard Oil was charged with at least 1,500 counts of violating antitrust laws and other charges. This became the process of regrouping the American oil industry which Standard Oil Company also made way for a massive restructuring of various businesses. This became the establishment of Exxon Corporation, Mobil Oil, Chevron Corporation, Marathon Oil Corporation and other smaller business resources. This was due to their monopoly control of business with oil and gas commodities throughout 12 different states ranging from New Jersey, Ohio, California, and other states. This also included more than 20 chemical, manufacturing, and pipe line companies which included South Penn Oil Company becoming Pennzoil which is now part Shell Oil Company.

Over the years approaching the 1st decade of 2000, the expansion of monopolized businesses with increasingly large markets, and investment concerns in America has consisted of massive industry conflicts. These are industries were people depend on products and services that became vital within issues like public safety, and cost. Understanding a major problem in America various executives and their corporate businesses have used the stability of income earnings from public utility monopolized companies for their own logic of greed. Considering this logic of greed the format of stable investments, productive business growth, and compliance within the U.S. Anti-Trust laws became vital conditions of resource. This is part of the understanding that provides an equation of opportunities for all businesses that are part of the governed discipline that provides a fair and resourceful expansion of the American economy.

As transportation, public utilities, agriculture, and banking expanded; the United States partly lead the way in creating U.S. Anti-Trust laws similar to the Separation of Powers in the American system of government. This concern with the Separation of Powers means that no one branch of government is more powerful than the other, but small, large, and or corporate American businesses can be conditionally different. Contrary to this fact business apart from government can respectfully perform various business activities as they try to achieve prosperous earnings, and growth. Besides these businesses that are most times monopolies with various, expensive equipment, they also consist of diversified levels of competition.

The consolidation of industry in America occasionally became the sad conflict of control that Enron with Kenneth Lay, WorldCom with Bernard Ebbers, and others had found within 10s of billions of dollars of corporate cash reserves. Observing a corporations cash reserves, and various business monopolies, these public utility issues also operate corporate economic values for contingent liabilities such as anti-trust disputes. Contrary to these issues of liability this became a level of cost which can be extensive unless they are making an unlawful effort to monopolize, or reduce competition in a certain market. This is part of the reason that Senator John Sherman, and the U.S. Congress established the Sherman Antitrust Act which became a set of laws to litigate against bad business issues of market control. Therefore as the top level management of corporations like Enron, WorldCom, Ameritech, and a few others made unlawful or bad decisions this provided certain agreements of conflict that "partly" led to economic disaster.

Monopoly businesses such as Microsoft Corporation, Seagate Technologies, and others that are gaining additional advancements with percentages of various markets in a lawful and innovative way are an exception to responsible business in America. These issues of business "by-products or parts" are usually working along a fine line of corporate procedures that observe most U.S. Patent Rights, and U.S. Anti-Trust law conditions of resource. Then theoretically a fair resource of business activities is a required legal equation. Understanding this business equation apart from banking, various public utilities, and a few other monopolies who invest in equipment with "patent rights" become resourceful and productive in business not to allow a complete failure. An appropriate example can be observed in the banking industry during 2007 with the failure of some of America's oldest investment banks like Lehman Brothers, Bear Stearns, and a few others. These businesses consisted of a-point-of-no-return or resulted in an incapable restructuring condition of existence.

In other anti-trust monopoly concerns like WorldCom Corporation their ambition became a logic to be more powerful, and financially aggressive in business then American Telephone and Telegraph Corporation. The Enron Corporation's problem with a few others is that they tried to control some of the smallest to largest electric utility companies in America after a short time in business. These activities where not comparable to the century old concept of business monopolies, that provided liable utilities. Observing these management and labor issues over 2 centuries was part of an expanding American population, and society. This societal issue consisted of good, bad, and a diversion of productive businesses that had to learn to operate or adjust their business activities under certain law conditions. Understanding this throughout certain markets in America various corporate businesses became issues of trying to acquire other businesses to become the largest monopoly, or a controlling corporate business. Some of these businesses ended up with bad operating standards of providing certain products, and or services.

Considering the 1990s, and up to 2007 with too big to fail corporate businesses and banks a U.S. Anti-Trust law era was observed with critical evaluations. This concern consisted of a variation of businesses that tried to become the largest industry leaders in the United States, and or the world conditionally "overnight". A brief list of companies involved in these "corporate transactions" that instantly failed or immediately needed restructuring was Enron Corporation, WorldCom Corporation, the proposed Sprint/WorldCom transaction, AOL-Time Warner Inc., and a few others. Another list of market controlling companies that expanded with productive or conflicting potential was ConocoPhillips, ExxonMobil, ArcelorMittal, BP-Amoco (BP), and a few others.

The most conflicting international and U.S. concerns of corporate businesses were ArcelorMittal Steel with their CEO Lakshmi Mittal whom is from India. Mittal Steel with the purchase of Inland Steel, and Bethlehem Steel having a foreign owner, and board members from the Middle East gave the U.S. government some national security concerns. This is part of the legal discipline that the U.S. government within the U.S. Federal Trade Commission, and the U.S. Department of Defense had established within conditional values observing congressional laws about U.S. defense contractors. These issues are part of American Defense contract requirements that these steel companies formerly engaged in during various times with a majority of American ownership.

Contrary to U.S. Defense contracts, and U.S. Federal Trade Commission issues British Petroleum (BP), and the complex activity of Sprint Corporation were reviewed, and argued in various government concerns. This consisted of difficulties ranging from liabilities to certain conflicting issues or business partners whom wanted to control certain markets. BP as it applies to Amoco Oil, and Mittal observing Inland Steel & Bethlehem Steel had been valuable American businesses. Understanding them, becoming foreign international monopolies owned, and operated in and out of the United States, this therefore had a tax revenue equation affecting the American system of government operating funds. As this accumulated into other corporate local, state, and federal government budget concerns, these economic values started to suffer problems which caused the layoff of public, private, business, and government employees.

Sprint Corporation making the effort to control a high percentage of long distance telephone services, and wireless communication telephone and internet services consisted of a lawfully aggressive level of responsible work. Contrary to ArcelorMittal, and BP as foreign owned businesses the Sprint Nextel Corporation, and a few other

American owned businesses consisted of a level of prosperity as they continued into their environment of U.S. Anti-Trust law concerns. These business issues also had U.S. Constitutional law values for government requirements, and the fairness of American business people in mind for U.S. domestic, and some foreign business antitrust law violation concerns.

Occasionally issues of U.S. Anti-Trust laws must be reviewed, and or recognized with lawful planning. This even more includes the fact that some good, and bad foreign business people may work to control large and expensive American corporate businesses. These issues also include some national security concerns. Therefore understanding this as it applies to international telecommunication companies that exist with capable control to the internet these become legal issues that are contingent upon lawful or conflicting business. Then the American system of government appropriated their leadership within officials, and business level concerns as CEO's, and lower levels of management had a responsibility to be elite. This was vital even if the lower management values survived or failed.

The U.S. domestic and international resource of telecommunication, communication, and media industry issues became conventional with wireless, and wired communication corporate businesses. Telecommunication issues have shifted from household telephone use to individual wireless use by a massive amount of customers that also conditionally use handheld devises for the internet. The communication industry within the media that includes newspaper issued products, news that is provided on television which includes the internet, and the overall combination of these services are part of rapidly changing markets. As time has prevailed a diversified resource of upgrades is observed with various products that have created a market of tremendous change, and innovation. These factors are also important to the issue that the 1st and 2nd decade of 2000 is still part of a devastating economic, and social time of distress apart from "monopolies or public utilities" to a vast amount of Americans.

Upon the agreement and corporate name Sprint Nextel Corporation these combined businesses operated as a company that takes on anti-trust business concerns, and risky chances with astute values of discipline. The last two CEO's of Sprint Nextel Corporation (c/o 2005) with Daniel Hesse, and Gary Foresee have been part of numerous communication combined mergers which they managed most times in the right direction. These are valuable business activities upon which most times these transactions are pivotal, or they are a workable parallel process to the Federal Communication Commission guild lines, U.S. Anti-Trust laws, the Securities and Exchange Commission, and other government legal requirements. This is also sometimes a basic format of lobbing government, but the people must survive financially with economic prosperity.

Contrary to the product, and service agreements that Sprint Nextel Corporation provides to 10s of millions of their subscribed customers, their active discipline to work with government (c/o even citizens) has been a major factor of a secured company. Randall Stephenson whom at this time is the CEO of American Telephone & Telegraph Corporation (AT&T) has some of the same responsibilities. These are business duties, and activities that AT&T holds in their monopoly resource of corporate values throughout this challenging, and upgrading market of innovative issues.

Observing the telephone and communication markets of America is part of the changing times upon which a vast amount of items are researched, and developed as patents become vital for lawful use. As America, and other countries have wireless communication systems the News Corporation, and their subsidiary "News Of The World" was quickly shutdown after decades of business. This was due to a "cell phone hacking scandal" of obtaining information illegally. This is the observation that the concentration of Rupert Murdoch's media business has various good, and some conditionally bad people throughout the company that him, and a few others don't seem to be able to manage with lawful discipline. This too big to manage business operating concern became the issues of law that on occasions the news media has a controlling level of business activities. These are activities that harm the people, and society in numerous ways that must be corrected. Contrary to this conflict they do provide millions of people with vital, and informative news, therefore their product, and service is important.

The understanding of an international conglomerate or massive media business which is a monopolized or controlling operation within similar concerns of Rupert Murdoch's media giant has seem to become an antitrust issue worldwide. Contrary to the good that is conditionally evident with humanity values there comes a time when this should be observed, and reviewed with some enforcement that a company may have too much control over certain technology markets, and people internationally. This is relevant to the excessive need, and requirement demands of products (c/o services) that become dependable to the people in America, and throughout the world. Understanding these issues over the years, and decades of regulating international monopolies may become an important factor of logical business concern in the future.

McDonald's Corporation and Kentucky Fried Chicken are corporate American fast food restaurants that hold worldwide market conditions similar to a monopoly. Contrary to these mega corporate fast food franchises the media giant within News Corporation is carefully considered an issue similar to these franchises. These are businesses that usually have more discipline within their operating business values of resources. Then they become important for the lawful discipline within respecting antitrust law values, but also providing local international communities with jobs, and sometimes a new way to operate in a high turnover rate of business. Observing these businesses that hold a strong controlling presents in their markets, the concept of antitrust law issues vaguely come up due to their valued business planning, and decision making as they most times lawfully compete with others.

The equation of conflict that is considered as an international monopoly becomes an issue of decisions within a government redress similar to the concern of Apple Inc., and other comparable companies whom find their products being copied. Then this applies if McDonald's Corporation finds their business becoming a force that changes to many rules, or they abuse people as it applies to the indifference of laws in various countries. The monopolized discipline of Kentucky Fried Chicken has occasional arguments with human, and animal rights groups which means all these companies have different issues that are part of their managing duties. This is where American and international laws can be applied in diversified ways without a reduction factor of good and prosperous business. How lawfully productive the company is; then this determines their value of acceptance to local or national standards of operation. Therefore various business values of quality are then recognized.

As American corporate businesses lead, and take on the concept of international monopolies, a logical factor within the concept of the United Nations (UN), and the United States government has increasingly consist of national security, and antitrust enforcement duties. Other resourceful countries then become an issue of governed liability. Some of these internationally involved countries are England, Europe, Russia, Australia, China, and occasionally Africa with India as a rising level of concern. These monopoly concerns include so many other countries (c/o over 180 UN members) of internationally governed values is part of what keeps foreign relations on close to one page of a good understanding.

Germany is also a tremendous factor within their technological base of developing mechanical processes. Contrary to Germany's technology base a moral condition of government, and business must be maintained for a well-respected society which applies to people, and government. Therefore even as this is observed in places like Indonesia (c/o GE light bulbs) with heavy industry this includes various American companies operating at low cost conditions internationally. Then these concerns must be astute with business, and government values of discipline.

Understanding the U.S. and more so international antitrust law concerns European regulators strongly rejected a proposed merger of WorldCom Corporation, and Sprint Corporation. This proposed merger during October of 1999 was valued at $129 billion dollars, and would have made these combined companies the largest telecommunication company ahead of the American Telephone & Telegraph Corporation. Observing this antitrust law factor exist worldwide within most well developed countries other than the United States, these issues of corporate merger, and buyout activity to establish a monopoly became serious legal issues of business, and government.

The concept of International Business Machine (IBM) became slightly an active issue of U.S. Anti-Trust concerns. Observing the IBM legal case issue of antitrust law conditions when they started to control the markets for personal computers, the only other issue was is IBM maintaining their business under the American system of U.S. Anti-Trust laws? In the case of the United States vs. IBM this case lasted for 13 years between 1969, to 1982 with a ruling of dismissal. Therefore the U.S. government may have spent a bit much on this argument, which also cost IBM a conditional amount of money.

American On Line Inc (AOL), and Time Warner Inc was two combined communication companies that merged (c/o AOL as a major buyout shareholder), and then split up due to a financial diversion. Their (Time Warner) business lead by AOL was a conditional resource of market ambition apart from long term business stability and planning. Observing this AOL was on its way to becoming a U.S. domestic, and international monopoly during the 1990s, but their business progress in this arbitrary market did not hold stability. Also their long-term economic and service discipline was no comparison to their new found buyout target of Time Warner Incorporated.

Understanding AOL and their brief success of extraordinary earnings with the company and stock worth over $220 billion dollars, this gave them extensive leveraging power from the banks. This also gave their CEO Steve Case a working concern of business expansion, and the awareness of an antitrust array of corporate issues. This was the understanding, and format of AOL becoming the parent company to Netscape with governed legal business concerns which consisted of government requirements, and the legal case of the United States vs. Microsoft Corporation.

The Microsoft Corporation legal case with Bill Gates being interrogated on the witness stand was an argument that Microsoft violated the Sherman Antitrust Act of 1890 due to the sale of certain computer software. This U.S. federal court hearing and case during 1998 was pursued by Joel Klein as the U.S. lead prosecutor. Also the judge was Thomas Penfield Jackson upon which Netscape provided loads of documents, and testimony evidence. It was determined on November 5, 1999 that Microsoft Corporation had manipulated various programs to sell all types of software, but the internet format of buying this software was extremely maintained to the advantage of Microsoft Corporation, and not Netscape, and others.

This array of corporate issues like AT&T contrary to Time Warner Inc. is valued with their arbitrary business expansion values of manageable corporate discipline. AOL was not an extensive legal subject of an antitrust law suit or argument, but as the DOT COM expansion of businesses went through conflicting times various issues became apparent. Observing the enormous amount of money invested, and upon which Netscape, and AOL's earnings suffered conflicts, and losses the DOT Com bubble had found a large hole. This applied concern existed as Steve Case (c/o AOL), and James Barkesdale the founder of Netscape both where tremendously close industry allies, and "Internet Browser" competitors with Microsoft Corporation. Then they had to figure out this new market with restructuring details, and logical business decisions.

The consolidation of the DOT COM industry of computers with equipment and software also included AOL's duties as a parent company to Netscape. This combination of business matters, with Netscape have been considered by AOL as the more inexpensive internet service provider. AT&T (c/o Lucent Technologies Inc. & Bell Laboratories) with AOL, Netscape, and others like Novell, and Hayes Communications as DOT COM corporations consisted of various business sectored issues. These where businesses competing, and working on industry standards like the advancements of computer modems, and then this was incorporated into a creation of the internal modem discipline.

The largest corporate business's that manufactured and controlled the resourceful operation of communication, and computer modem activity was AT&T, IBM, and Novell. Considering the U.S. Dept of Defense having partly developed the multiplex system, and modems which no one company has monopolized on, this vital by-product has become part of all computers to connect to the internet. Therefore this has been a critical process for AOL, Netscape, and others within them working together for controlling various internet percentages of certain sectors of business, and markets.

Another observed factor is that these markets in America expanded tremendously with a generation of old, and young American people becoming computer literate. Then as it applies to a worldwide market of telecommunication, communication, and media industry concerns, an uncontrollable resource of market issues became legal issues of importance. In this expanding DOT COM market various people's personal and confidential information, along with the content nature of pitchers and filming for the viewing audience became an issue. Also this then appropriates the valued concern of needing a legal, legislative, social, and a business format of lawful and moral discipline.

The expanded use of computers, cell phones, and the internet became what was considered the DOT COM bubble with business owning investors like Ted Turner, numerous investment bankers, other valued citizens, and various professionals. With large investments from Ted Turner, and other venture capital investors AOL achieved additional liquidity success, and then became prime victim to conflicting market activity. In other concerns this was considered a troubled economic example of a busted bubble. These are industry values in America that the U.S. government was only slightly prepared for within the Federal Communication Commission, the Federal Trade Commission, and other resource government concerns. Therefore observing AOL, and a few other businesses some investors took hard losses which included Ted Turner contrary to some other investments that paid off investors well.

Observing other major conflicting resources of concern the arbitration of various business trade groups such as within developing, and manufacturing technology devices became discretionary in various good, and some bad ways. This was recognized by certain people with the Securities and Exchange Commission, and the U.S. Department of Justice with their "Anti-Trust" Division whom responded with litigation slowly at first. Their slow response to such an aggressively moving, and changing atmosphere of technology, and businesses was part of them combining the understanding of these industry issues of concern. Then the American peoples use, and the law binding existence of legislature with the establishing of laws for the people became an issue that could be consistent with the U.S. Constitution.

Besides the U.S. Anti-Trust divisions of the U.S. Dept. of Justice the government must take, and work from complaints, but also recognize when antitrust laws are threatening to citizens, and or businesses, and how these types of laws are potentially being violated. The economic factor of long term monopolies like with utility companies or the control of pharmaceutical companies with values of discipline went through the DOT COM troubles, and market turmoil with some value of stability. This was also the concern of technology products with more, computer operating speed to get, receive, or send information. Therefore computers became user friendly, and this even includes spending money to buy new and used items to be sent to the consumers. Then contrary to the internet service fees, this sometimes consisted of fraudulent activities which become another problem to consumers.

The factor of newly found internet issues of fraud, and crime has been causing people to take some economic losses in various ways which consisted of a government need to improve. Contrary to this fact a vast amount of time with enormous amounts of people, and businesses making good of this new found technology has changed how some shopping, education, dating, banking, and other things are done in America. Understanding the fact that the United States has numerous monopolies, and the activity of small and large businesses including corporations with the use of technology is still part of an important, and prosperous money, and tax revenue circulation. Therefore this factor of America has helped some resources become an even more well-developed society. Then theoretically these values within the changing times still consist of caution, and clear observation within America maintaining its values of a well-established and forward moving nation of discipline.

CHAPTER THREE

Public Utilities In America

An American Study Of Business & Monopolies

Public Utilities In America

The American system of public utility companies, and their business markets are a vital resource within public health, convince of liable standards, and a compounding diversified issue of economic, and financial values. This becomes the consolidated excess of tens of millions of American households, various facilities, and businesses with water, wastewater, gas, electric, and other utilities like telephone, and the internet providing various service agreements. These public utilities became dependable services with certain detail suggested products throughout most all businesses, residential, and even government customers paying for these appropriate services.

Observing 2013 between Steven Chu as the U.S. Department of Energy Secretary, and Julius Genachowski as the Chairman of the Federal Communication Commission their duties are vital to America as a well-developed society. This becomes the managing duties of their administrative employees with other departments that apply to the people, industry values within most public utility monopolies, and some scientific values of technology that may include water reclamation. Also them, and others have conditionally reviewed new technology issues like "Renewable Energy", Fossil Energy, Nuclear Energy, Solar Energy, Cell Phones, Text Messages, Broadband, and the Internet. Another vital factor in America is recognized with the infrastructure which includes diversified utility equipment, and even the upgrading of storm water levees, hydroelectric dams, and various bridges.

Considering a logical format of business, every livable region of America has access to valuable public utility resources as the citizen's base of people, and businesses are chosen, and designated as regional consumers. This is a conditional value of how the best inventions, products, and services with economic values have provided the American society with basic utility necessities. During the 1st decade of 2000 these issues of public utilities have become conditional with a high cost like within fatal coal mining accidents, and gas explosions. These are the commodities within coal fired energy plants, the oil and gas production industry, and a few other scientific studies and subjects which helps various public utilities, and some public policy duties with logical requirements. This also becomes the foundation of these market controlling businesses providing valuable services, and their discipline to generate billions of dollars annually.

A productive public utility company, consist of people trained properly, and with some ambitious employees to be productive working with various oil, gas, electrical, and water distribution systems. Also this includes cable television, telephone and internet services with various companies that manage office, field, and plant operations on a day by day level of duty. Then these vital assets include equipment that they have usually made good on for their services with their invested dollars in business. Observing, these industry values and standardize services this business discipline consist of some conditional and factual resources of liability, and economic factors. Therefore as a monopoly; these public utility sectors today most times stand apart or astute from various antitrust laws.

The business within public utility companies in America is governed with various laws that equate industry discipline. A formal logic within laws starts with the Sherman Antitrust Act of 1890 which became the lawful discipline for excessive control of businesses. This law established that non-public utility businesses should not control other businesses, but also how regional public utilities, and other businesses cannot control certain people, smaller businesses, and markets unlawfully to become monopolies.

Another law, consist of the Public Utility Holding Company Act of 1935 which became important with the logical equation of investment issues that helped public utility companies expand. This has kept certain corporations, and individuals similar to Samuel Insull whom during the 1920s was an innovator, and investor from Britain living in America as a person who made progress in public utility developments. He became aggressive in controlling unregulated monopolies like most Midwest regional electrical public utility business firms. Samuel Insull held large public utility investments as Holding Companies which included his valued ownership in electrical infrastructure upgrades. This existed in Northwest Indiana (c/o NIPSCO), and more so in the Chicago, Illinois electric utility market before losing most of his life savings, and investments in the 1929 stock market crash.

As these business issues became observant today the U.S. Congress passed the Public Utility Holding Company Act of 2005, and the Energy Policy Act of 2005. These factual congressional issues with debates became vital to create an Energy Policy which some of these legislative values gave the Federal Energy Regulatory Commission a limited amount of regulatory authority. Considering the U.S. Department of Energy was established in 1977 (c/o the Jimmy Carter Presidential administration) throughout this 36 year time span, a resourceful Energy Policy has only been established 3 times.

Certain "Energy Policy" mandated rules were established from the factor of the Federal Power Act, and the Rivers and Harbor Act of the United States government. These policy matters consisted of needing a permit to navigate streams, and build various types of dams. The U.S. Congress left this authority of regulating dams, and navigational waters up to the state government. Therefore as the state was required to hold the permit from the federal government, these responsibilities occasionally got more complex. Then sometimes the permit process became slow with funding, and this consisted of a detailed industry regulating process from government.

Besides the fact that energy inventions, and dam projects go back almost 100 years these changing times required the insight of various government departments. These departments have been the U.S. Department of Energy (DOE), the U.S. Department of Interior (DOI), the U.S. Department of Labor (DOL), and various individual state utility regulators. These tremendously changing times with utility companies and hydroelectric dams have created the need for these advancing technologies to have more government attention, awareness, and appropriately enforced regulation.

Even today with the leadership of the DOI's secretary Ken Salizar, and the DOE secretaries from Spenser Abraham up to Steven Chu wind farms have been established for energy throughout various parts of the United States. This latest, and newest expansion has been an issue of conservation that consist of renewable energy, and or clean energy which has caused an enormous amount of wind farms to be an inclusive part of Americas infrastructure. Also this includes massive solar energy sites and projects. These newly built wind farms consist of advanced wind mill technology, and this includes other American energy experts making compared advancements in nuclear energy, and solar energy.

Observing public utility companies with investors that have enormous corporate assets that are complex, the issue of liability to customers, and the workers is vital. This includes how they provide service to these systems as this industry holds too much leveragability for the large financial conflicts they can cause. An appropriate example is the $5.5 billion dollar issue of damage during the Northeast American electrical blackout in 2003. This means that the government has expanded legislative disciplines with these types of businesses in "the future" that must be effective, and productive.

Unlike Samuel Insull not having the highest "utility and business" standards, these issues have recently become similar to a more secured banking industry. Contrary to similar banking investments the industry of American public utilities also holds too many professional values, or levels of domestic, and or national security concerns that must be protected. These concerns exist for certain levels of precaution "not" to be considered without safety, secured regulation, and logical professional standards of legislature for responsible values of discipline. Also these issues consist of resources of liability to not be strictly governed, and protected by the United States without liability disciplines for all customers, and citizens. Therefore it is important for these industries to be some of the most reliable resources to citizens, and government without bad decision making.

Most monopolized businesses are slightly different from those like the American Water Works Company, Tennessee Valley Authority (TVA), Pacific Gas & Electric (PG&E), Arizona Public Service Company (APS), Northern Indiana Public Service Company (NIPSCO), Entergy Corporation, and a host of others. Then a similar value of importance is relevant with the Edison franchise of companies consisting of Southern California Edison, Commonwealth Edison of Chicago (ComEd), Consolidated Edison of New York (ConEd), Detroit Edison (now DTE Energy), and a few others. Therefore these diversified, but similar utility companies operate in different geographical regions which includes diversified weather conditions, and state law regulatory values. These become the vital factors of what makes some regional public utilities different from others, and their professional disciplines to offer certain utility services that are astute with liability.

The U.S. Department of Energy is commissioned with the duty to oversee the regulated activity of electric, and gas public utilities which occasionally includes hydroelectric dams in America. A factual issue of common logic, consist of these companies as public utility electric companies which are connected considering this was observed during the Northeast American blackout of August 2003. As it applies to this day in time the 2003 blackout was factored from a diversified amount of electric utility companies within an electrical grid that includes a SCADA system. A "SCADA" system failure was one major blame for this massive electrical outage, and not likely an excuse like a "tree" falling on electrical equipment or disturbing a utility line.

This SCADA system argument was the most logical considering that this system controls a majority of their mechanical and more so electrical equipment that is applicable to most all electrical component processes. Observing this the SCADA control panel, and system considering the Northeast blackout problem consisted of Edison franchises, and utility companies like FirstEnergy Corporation. The corporation FirstEnergy whom was part of the blame of this critical electrical power distribution failure is like some others that did not care to keep high standards within people that were productive. Then as it applies to this fact they were not productive during their tenure of productive professional observation.

Spencer Abraham whom was Secretary of the U.S. Department of Energy was guided to the determined factor that FirstEnergy Corp should not need to be punished for their faulty part in the massive 2003 blackout. Contrary to these factual issues of public utility liability this also meant better operating standards needed to be applied. Observing the issue that this blackout affected 8 American states (Oh, Mi., NY, Ma, NJ, Pa, Vt., Ct.), and 2 Canadian provinces provides appropriate concern for various duties to improve professionally. This becomes the logic that public utility companies, the American system of government, and the citizens have a vital duty to work together. Then therefore logical citizens and national security are vitally considered as all conditions of business, and government are evaluated for the best solutions, and factors of the American society.

The diversion of public utilities with patents, are slightly different from market controlling business monopolies. These issues are observed from the control of popular products, and values of

Standard Oil Company (c/o Amoco-BP), the consideration of News Corporation, Microsoft Corporation, and American Telephone & Telegraph Corporation with Ameritech. As it applies to AT&T with some of their gracefully good, and conditionally bad attempted transactions this was observed when they considered the multi-billion dollar purchase of T-Mobile. Considering patent's, and antitrust law arguments this was valued for small expanding businesses although some may say T-Mobile is not as large as others, but their expanded business resources had been appropriately apparent. Therefore even as some American government officials inadvertently supported an enemy foreign agenda, certain businesses before the 9-11 Report attacks consisted of U.S. Constitutional law concerns, and other legal concerns that should have been considered as well.

Some of these issues intervened with the tenure of Bill Richardson as the Secretary of the U.S. Department of Energy which included a sense of global business expansion concerns. These corporate businesses and other international businesses became issues of bad or conflicting international outsourcing of American jobs. Also between Mexico, and the Middle East with some foreign engineering, and design professionals (c/o President Bill Clinton) America suffered in diversified ways. This also was a loss of American engineering, and industry values of professionalism. Therefore then the infrastructure, and the industrial base of businesses like utilities, and manufacturing suffered. These years (c/o the late 1990s) became a point and time when individual states consisted of major social problems like fatal accidents, crime, and terrorism which conditionally kept other Americans from being productive.

Understanding the fact that various corporate businesses are not public utilities similar to their monopolized markets, this becomes the diversified responsibility of government to equate certain massive business activities. This is the value of how American Telephone & Telegraph Corporation (AT&T) had to restructure in the mid-1980s from being dismantled to reorganize under U.S. Anti-Trust laws, and other legal disciplines established by the United States government. These are a few factors of how AT&T and a variation of other valued businesses can have an economic effect on the American economy. Therefore contrary to the contributions, of Alexander Graham Bell, and Thomas Edison a vast amount of Americans have worked for decades making these service controlling monopoly businesses liable, and helpful. This then became a responsible market to the people for a logical cost to most all facilities.

The American managing issue of resourceful business, and values of professional, and government engineering are vital to public utilities, and the infrastructure. These issues apply to various businesses, and facilities in tremendous ways upon which they are closely regulated by the American system of government. Understanding this value of concern most all facilities including government pays some type of utility bill along with all commercial and residential customers. Then the infrastructure throughout the United States has a vital foundation that government tax revenue helps to keep up to date. Observing these losing issues of professionalism which have hit record low points in the American society, the people, and a variation of property have suffered from damages that hold a high cost. So even with the high mortgage foreclosure rate (c/o 2007 to 2011) with the other parts of this equation including houses, and business properties being damaged from inadequate care which has been part of an obsolete or unmanaged infrastructure. This additional cost is effective to homeowners, insurance companies, and the U.S. government.

An enormous amount of government and engineering issues of failure in America was observed with the 2005 Hurricane Katrina in New Orleans, Louisiana and some other states. This consisted of obsolete concrete levees surrounding New Orleans from the Gulf of Mexico that collapsed. As soon as the levees collapsed a tremendous level of water from the Gulf of Mexico flowing onto the land caused destruction to large amounts of people, and property throughout the 9th Ward of New Orleans. This could have been prevented by Mayor Ray Nagan's administration of engineering professionals providing good inspections, and then upgrading this obsolete infrastructure problem. Observing the George Bush, and then Barack Obama administration this has been a slow process until "disaster occurs" that needs scheduled reviews, inspections, and workable solutions of discipline with local municipalities.

This infrastructure problem became tremendously conflicting to public utility companies like Entergy Corporation of New Orleans that was hit with enormous damage during Hurricane Katrina. Considering

Entergy Corp provides electric utility services to New Orleans, and a few other nearby southern regional states they have had to work to restructure throughout business, and government with argumentative conditions of resource. Even the Sewerage and Water Board of New Orleans with the U.S. Army Corps of Engineers should have recognized this problem before the U.S. military was commissioned to help the city before, and severely after this tremendous hurricane. Therefore unlike the Hurricane Katrina disaster (c/o Entergy, and other utility concerns) within those cities, towns, and state government regulatory concerns them, and a few others created a continuous format of upgrading the infrastructure. Then these upgrades from damage became safe, secure, and efficient public utility service resources once again.

As regional Americans observe valuable electric public utilities such as Tennessee Valley Authority (TVA), and various Edison Company franchises the 2 most conflicting utility companies have recently been Pacific Gas & Electric (PG&E), and Portland General Electric. These public utility companies have consisted of numerous conditions of concern even as they have encountered tuff economic values, and liability issues in their markets. Portland GE became a well-developed electric utility company that was a concept of financial leverage through various banks which even more so occurred when Enron Corporation became their parent company of ownership in a corporate buyout. Considering these factors the combination of Enron Corporation taking over Portland GE gave Enron Corporation additional leverage on assets with various banks including their business relationship with Citigroup Incorporated.

Following the Enron Corporation of Houston, Texas scandal Portland General Electric had suffered financially along with other Enron assets, investors, and employees. The longest serving employees (c/o 15 to 20 plus years) of Portland General Electric had lost at least 75% of their pension retirement savings. Some of these employee retirement pension accounts consisted of years of service which gave each of them a value at over $100,000.00 and in less than 5 years that amount fell below less than $5,000.00. This level of corporate business with Kenneth Lay and others at Enron Corporation was a factor of greed to control more cash liquidity. Also this included PG&E as Enron pursued their corrupt business activity with these and various public utility companies which became conflicting to state government regulators like in California.

Contrary to certain financial crime issues, fatal negligence was observed with Pacific Gas & Electric (PG&E) which they were the cause of a 2010 San Bruno, California "gas explosion" with a death toll of 8 people. As this PG&E gas explosion consisted of damage that destroyed, and leveled 35 houses, this is a rare problem that must be professionally prevented. The cause of this explosion was due to obsolete gas distribution equipment that was considered for utility upgrading, but these where issues that became an ongoing level of procrastination. Even as the financial funding was there for this gas utility upgrading process, it was not completed to comply, and operate with safety standards. With around 100 lawsuits filed against PG&E, and the state government restructuring from the Enron Corp (bankruptcy & fraud) legal issues, these and other corporate problems continued to produce losses. Then these businesses along with WorldCom Corporation became some the most tremendous losses to the American society for public utility companies, and the people in recent times.

Over the decades up to 2003 Tennessee Valley Authority (TVA) has made conditional advancements especially as they have some comparison values to Commonwealth Edison of Chicago, Consolidated Edison of New York, Southern California Edison, and a few others. The difference is that Tennessee Valley Authority is a U.S. government owned-independent corporation that was established to provide navigation, flood control, electricity generation and distribution. Also TVA is active in fertilizer manufacturing, and economic development which on occasions consist of overseeing various projects that is partly supervised by the U.S. Army Corps of Engineers.

Tennessee Valley Authority with their headquarters in Knoxville, Tennessee has worked to establish various large projects which TVA has ownership of numerous flood control dams, and hydroelectric dam projects. This also includes equipment that is set up for interstate commerce of electrical power distribution which as it applies to TVA provides their services to numerous states. The first dam under the authority of TVA was the Wilson Dam which was completed in 1924, but was authorized in 1933 with the signing of the Tennessee Valley Authority Act by Franklin D. Roosevelt. Decades later TVA grew to establish 28 more flood control dams, and hydroelectric dams, 11 coal fired energy plants, and then this made them the largest electric utility company in the United States.

TVA service areas are most of Tennessee, portions of Alabama, Mississippi, and Kentucky which includes small parts of Georgia, North Caroline, and Virginia. Considering these southeastern Mid-Atlantic states the geographical setting consist of tree covered mountains with electrical transmission towers and cables running into the highest parts of various mountains. Also these small, and large cities including isolated towns which are spread throughout the region became part of this grid for electricity, irrigation, and navigation within flood control. These many regional business values outline some factors of why during 2009 TVA had revenue earnings of $11.26 billion dollars.

Another level of activity that was eliminated over the years throughout the valley region of Tennessee has been their U.S. Department of Defense work at Oak Ridge, Tennessee which goes back to certain developments within the Manhattan Project. Since the 1940s up to 2013 with their recent CEO Tom Kilgore the utility business resource of Tennessee Valley Authority has become more active in nuclear energy upon which they have built, and manage 3 nuclear energy plants. This was a process they created over the years within their American experience of researching, and developing nuclear technology into energy plants. Also these technology disciplines were converted from the 1945 World War II Oak Ridge, Tennessee war time production of the atom bomb. This war time resource of items, and technology was outlawed by the U.S. Atomic Energy Commission (AEC) as part of nuclear proliferation after World War II with the establishing disciplines of the United Nations. Therefore this is also factual to a vast amount of activities by the U.S. Army Corps of Engineers especially as it applies to east of the Mississippi River.

The Mississippi River has been the bench mark of flood control developments, and of many dams, and river lock system projects. Also the Mississippi River is the dividing point of government regulation, and managing between the U.S. Army Corps of Engineers, and the U.S. Bureau of Reclamation which both go back to the 1880s. Every type of dam east of the Mississippi River is the authority of the Army

Corps of Engineers, and every type of dam west of the Mississippi River is the authority of the Bureau of Reclamation. One of the largest and most complex dams built in the United States, and authorized by the Bureau of Reclamation is the Hoover Dam which is west of the Mississippi between northern Arizona, and Nevada. The Hoover Dam is also a facility for irrigated water, electricity, and flood control from the Colorado River.

Observing the Hoover Dam with water controlled resources, and hydroelectric power system units it provides water, and electricity to various parts of America's southwestern states. The authority of the Hoover Dam provides electricity to at least 10 cities or towns in California including Los Angeles, and the Southern California Edison Company. Also this includes a good portion of electricity to Nevada, and Arizona. Major water resources are also applied to the Metropolitan Water District of Southern California from the professional and resourceful activity at the Hoover Dam.

As the Hoover Dam was built with Frank Crowe as the Superintendent and Bureau of Reclamation Engineer Walker Young between 1931 to 1936 (c/o the Great Depression), there where around 100 workers who died. Observing this good and conditionally bad concern, this issue gave way to new safety disciplines, and responsibilities. These good and bad government and industry concerns are factors to the improved safety standards of engineering design, and construction techniques within these, and similar construction sites, and projects. Therefore observing this the Bureau of Reclamation and the Army Corps of Engineers has constantly been involved in this project and others up to this day of 2013 with appropriate regulation that is helpful for American workers.

The U.S. Bureau of Reclamation today with their present Commissioner Michael Connor is different from the days of its beginning with Elwood Mead whom also worked on the Boulder Dam which was later known as the Hoover Dam. Upon the dam being named after President Hebert Hoover the Bureau of Reclamation was understood to be an agency within the U.S. Department of Interior. Their government duties of resourceful land, and water throughout the United States has constantly, and more so today became an issue for the people, mapping for all U.S. regions, and various public land concerns.

Another government value applied to public utilities is the Environmental Protection Agency. This agency throughout most American cities and towns have been aggressive on occasions by establishing more effective wastewater treatment processes, and municipal treatment plants. These wastewater process disciplines can put certain levels of water back into society for usable standards. Observing these standards is relevant for safe and logical conditions of water for natural resources such as watering land components like grass, and flowers. Then the normal logic of treated (effluent) water deposits are released into a river, or other waterway natural systems. This is even more so true at U.S. Steel Corporation (Gary Works Plant), and some major chemical companies who threat their own wastewater, and then reuse a certain amount of this vital commodity.

As wastewater and storm water treatment facilities, and issues occur with operating capacities throughout most all major cities in America this is a vital part of the infrastructure which includes numerous water company utilities. Water also as an important and accessible commodity in America most times is understood as a city, town, or regional business, and more so a municipal government duty of regulated value. This becomes the outline of every state government, and more than 95% of all cities, and towns in the United States which provides this utility service to all households, and businesses as an engineering, and public health value.

Most wastewater and storm water issues within various cities that reside near very active rivers, lakes, and even certain oceans usually manage their storm water concerns as a high priority. This was extremely conflicting during the 2008 floods of northwest Indiana, and Iowa considering this storm system first hit New Orleans, Louisiana. The Federal Emergency Management Agency (FEMA) became a very active government social concern, and economic factor during, and after this storm began as Hurricane Ike in the southern United States. Understanding this storm it caused various obsolete, and or incomplete infrastructure components of river levees to consist of cresting water levels. This tremendous water level occurred on the Little Calumet River in Northwest Indiana which flooded, and destroyed hundreds of homes, and business assets including facilities. Contrary to the various types of buildings that accumulated severe damage including a

NW Indiana University theater, other facilities where damaged under FEMA tragedy required disciplines.

In Des Moines, Iowa which is the capital city of the state of Iowa the citizens were devastated with flooding during the 2008 floods, and this came mostly from the cresting Des Moines River. Also there was water surrounding the Iowa State Capital Building which is where the Governor's office is located making access to this government facility very complex. Then the observation of other Iowa floods occurred in Cider Rapids from the Cider River which Alliant Energy Corp reported during this 2008 flood that electrical power would be terminated for a conditional amount of time. Alliant Energy Corporation is a holding company for Interstate Power and Light. Between the two they distribute electricity which includes the purchase and distribution of natural gas in Iowa, and Minnesota. Also Alliant Energy Corporation has its headquarters and is incorporation in Madison, Wisconsin which outlines the regional work that a public utility company must be liable for even during a State of Emergency.

Observing America's effort to overcome certain disasters with utility companies, and the people was a vital factor of the 2011 tornado that destroyed a vast amount of Joplin, Missouri. Concerning this the utilities was more than likely the last thing on most of their minds due to the fact that 158 people were killed in this city with a population of just under, 52,000 citizens. This goes along the line of Hurricane Sandy during 2012 that caused heavy damage to the east coast of the United States. The storm severely caused problems to the surroundings of New York City, New Jersey, and a few others in this Northeast American regional. The logical factor is that these regions of America will have to rebuild to a point that the infrastructure and public utilities can withstand these acts of nature with only minor or logical repairs. Therefore since no man can change these acts of nature, except but to serve and protect themselves, families, and assets the American infrastructure must be pivotal with stability. Then most all utilities must be updated to the best structural and operating standards.

As the collaboration of public utilities, local storm water, and wastewater issues are recognized as a business, and or government entity they are observed as dependable issues of professionalism which must be astute. This is valued in a massive level of cities throughout America with their public utility monopoly disciplines that are second nature with their responsibilities. Another level of responsibility is their effort to protect their overall public utility system, and their business in a lawful and logical way without trying to control other businesses. These values of resource also include Professional Codes of Conduct and standards that are a resource of good corporate business citizenship in a region. Therefore even as U.S. Anti-Trust laws apply these valued businesses become an important part of the U.S. economy, and service that a majority of citizens try hard to appreciate.

CHAPTER FOUR

Corporate Markets In America

An American Study Of Business & Monopolies

Corporate Markets In America

The massive concept of corporate markets in America upon which includes some values of monopoly businesses are a resource of economic, technical, and product values. These values such as their control of patents, recipes, rights of author, and or ingredients for products, and service agreements have been part of America becoming a well-developed society.

An enormous level of work from Henry Ford, Wilber Wright, Orville Wright, George Eastman, Alexander Bell, and others in a highly industrialized nation has held some of the most critical patents in America, and sometimes worldwide. These patents with production of products have been around since the early 1900s. Then with the most productive patents, inventions, production, and massive sales with disciplines of managing business the American industrial revolution prospered for millions of people.

Even some black Americans that did not have equal rights at one time made enormous contributions to America's industrial advancements. These people upon establishing assets consisted of George W Carver who experimented, and developed products made for various agriculture specimens like peanuts. Also John Johnson who created Ebony and Jet Magazines (c/o Johnson's Publishing Company) which have distributed publication products throughout America, and some parts of the world. Therefore as times, and contributing factors advanced from developing cars, airplanes, cameras, film, food, publications, and medicine these patents, products, and markets increased with lawful issues, and mass production.

Managing a corporation in America changed over the decades with more markets, patents, products, corporate businesses, and even corporate titles. This becomes the outline for their expanded business values, or how various businesses have been dissolved. During 2007, and 2008 this consisted of a vast amount of commerce banks, investment banks, and various large, and small businesses. Either direction this condition in America affects the economy even if it does not always show or is reflected from the point system of the Dow Jones Industrial Average.

As the Dow Jones Industrial Average does not reflect all American small, and large businesses, or corporations this stock market average has recently taken small movements of higher point gains to record levels in 2013. On the other side of these market resources more corporate businesses are closing their doors of operation for good. Although other business startups are being developed, some corporate businesses like Hostees Brands Incorporated whom started as Interstate Bakers Corporation have closed during the year 2012 due to bankruptcy, and union disputes. Understanding this becomes vital when large corporate businesses close which conditionally affects thousands of employees, and government tax revenue for all levels of the American system of government to operate.

Hostees Brands held a strong market position in baking, manufacturing, shipping, and selling their bakery goods to millions of customers. This became a prosperous consolidation of snack cakes, and brand name food items like Twinkie that were distributed all over the United States as strong conditions of marketable products. Then considering this company that has been in operation since the 1920s with their business disciplines to achieve profitable earnings, they had come to a losing economic struggle during 2009, and their final days of 2012. Therefore even as a vast amount of companies lose their business existence, and others are created the stock markets will continue to be held up by good, bad, and complex investors. Then the strongest corporate businesses of economic and production values usually prevail.

Within comparison throughout businesses of a corporate capacity Hostees Brands Inc, and the Hershey Foods Corporation have agriculture, and some monopolized business values with the financial resources to sale their products. Contrary to the Hostees Brands Inc issues of bankruptcy, and labor union disputes that were part of economic losses, the Hershey Foods Corporation has managed to keep productive sales and production cost financially balanced. One of the main differences is that Hershey Food Corporation is the largest chocolate manufacture in North America with their headquarters in Hershey, Pennsylvania. Considering this corporate observation the Hershey Company has a long history which includes aggressive disputes with labor unions, and local agriculture constituents. These were, and have become strong leadership values in American agriculture which lead to prosperous sales of chocolate, caramel, and now food products. These values have given them a percentage of various markets in America, and prosperous sales in some worldwide markets.

Various companies like Montgomery Ward's, Service Merchandise, Bear Stearns Investment bank, Lehman Brothers, various commerce banks, and other businesses have recently struggled through economic difficulties. These were decades to century old businesses that during the 1990s up through 2010 could not recover from various economic conditions in America. On the other side of business Apple Inc. Microsoft Corp, Kellogg Company, the three major American automobile companies of Ford, General Motors, and Chrysler are a small group of the American companies of viable business markets. Also Coca Cola Company and PepsiCo Incorporated are strong beverage companies that hold American, and worldwide markets as corporate America businesses that endured the good, and bad of economic times of the United States. Therefore this diversified resource of markets in America is outlined to the extent that there are problems affecting the economy that must be restructured with business, and government solutions for the people.

Market controlling businesses and monopolies have held stability in America from being a few years old "to some" existing for over a century. They have also tapped American and international markets with business disciplines similar to the Kellogg Company with their recent 2012 CEO John Bryant holding a strong portion of cereal sales in America, and most developed countries. Also United Parcel Service Inc (UPS) with their recent 2012 CEO Scott Davis has maintained strong sales, and earnings domestically, and internationally upon which they can travel, and ship packages to most parts of the world. As it applies to U.S. Anti-Trust laws these are service, and product industry business resources that don't easily hold conflict. These corporate businesses have decades of experience, and have managed assets including liquidity in their progressive business values. Therefore their discipline of liability and liquidity in all resources is part of their ability to control these markets.

During 2011 Kellogg Company held 30% of the American market of cereal sales, and 60% to 70% of the market in other developed countries. This is a challenging market which is based on the U.S.

Food and Drug Administration (FDA) standards. Understanding these publicly traded businesses, and various U.S. government standards this includes the Securities and Exchange Commission rules, regulation and laws of their overall resource of investments concerning business. Then this is usually part of the Kellogg Company, and some others with satisfying results between farmers, investors, employees, various corporate businesses, and the American system of government with all consumers. Considering these issues of business, and government the Kellogg Company has managed these levels of business production for over a century, and therefore a vast amount of experience, assets, liquidity, and appropriate resources have been crucial.

UPS also being a company that is over 100 years old has managed to deal with government legal standards that are provided by the United States Department of Transportation (DOT) in almost every resource of shipping cargo. With air, land, and water transportation being part of their ability of diversified package shipping, these disciplines include Scott Davis the UPS CEO (c/o 2011) to keep high, and low levels of management issues in order. Those management values consist of an enormous amount of sales, assets, operating liquidity, and the overall business operation. Also this is valuable in how they control their market share of business in America, and throughout the world. The business operation of UPS includes their more than 390,000 employees in 2011 which operates throughout 220 countries, and territories. Therefore this consisted of these business resource values, which is balanced on knowing the laws, rules, and regulation in America, and abroad. Then this includes some U.S. government regulation which is similar or mandated in other developed countries.

Apple Inc, Microsoft Corporation, General Electric Corporation, Raytheon Corporation, and a variation of businesses are different within how their product sales exist in a worldwide capacity. The cost of some of these products (c/o some services) are part of the affordability of a regions people considering what parts of the world these products do well in. These corporations have strong backgrounds within managing patents for all of their products which range from very old, to the newest patents as product items. Then Apple Inc, and Microsoft Corporation can be slightly understood as they have expanded over the last 20 years with an enormous amount of new patented products. Most of these products enter-phase between the arbitration of recently, established cell phones, digital cameras, computers, and software operating systems.

The concept and patents on digital camera technology (c/o microchips & memory cards) has become so tremendous that it has somewhat put Eastman Kodak film company nearly out of business during 2011 and 2012. In 1975 an Eastman Kodak engineer named Steven Sasson attempted to build a digital camera, but their prototype was too large, and was considered a technical exercise not created for production. Observing the Eastman Kodak Company failed to keep up with their many growing competitors like Fiji, Sony, GE, and a few others in January 2012 their Chairman & CEO Antonio Perez, and the company filed for Chapter 11 bankruptcy protection.

As the "Digital Camera" became a marketable product, this conditionally eliminated the need of Kodak film for most cameras. During the 1990s the CEO of Kodak George Fisher made productive attempts to work with Microsoft, and certain merchandisers which included conditional agreements with Apple Inc to gain part of the digital camera market. The next CEO of Kodak Daniel Carp made even stronger moves with various digital camera products which made them number 1 in this American category of items that managed to gain 40% of the market within 2005 sales of $5.7 billion dollars. Each year after their numbers began to drop compared to various companies observing this competitive market of expanding digital camera consumer interest. This was such an expanding, and critical time for the digital camera patents apart from film producing photos that various markets for cameras changed considerably. Therefore other companies apart from the Eastman Kodak Company used their money to expand with digital camera technology, and this gave them a prosperous edge.

During various digital camera developments from certain corporations this took a few years during the 1990s for full expansion. Contrary to Kodak other businesses like Fiji, Sony, General Electric, Canon, and others invested in this technology while Eastman Kodak was slow at the start of production. The Eastman Kodak Company was still focused on spending heavily on a diversified group of film products. These products which included an extensive film division of items with patents for developing film consisted of the good, and bad of photogenic paper which accumulated crucial issues with conflicts. Observing these products especially with the film business became discretionary considering the use of film was conditionally being phased out. Understanding this, the changing times where transforming a market that Americans valued, but now they had found, and adjusted to more advanced technology.

As it applies to General Electric Corporation, and Raytheon Corporation, contrary to Eastman Kodak, and now Eastman Chemical Company these corporate businesses do more direct contract work with the U.S. Department of Defense, NASA, NOAA, major utility companies, and others. Most times this becomes the establishment of newly found technology that became helpful. Considering most of these are expensive projects, during 2012 these companies have been more secluded apart from product advancements from Apple, and Microsoft due to the restructuring of the U.S. government budget, and the American economy.

Jeffery Immelt the present CEO of General Electric (GE) has worked closer with President Barrack Obama on a commission that promotes high tech jobs in America, but GE is still a conglomerate with many valuable products. This becomes a slight conflict observing President Obama's decisions to extremely reduce the budget of the National Aeronautics and Space Administration (NASA) which included eliminating the space shuttle program. These issues of research and development were a vital part of space exploration as it applies to adjustments on the earth in America. Therefore upon this fact a certain variation of technological studies with advancements were discontinued.

The loss of NASA is a tremendous conflict to American values of technological advancements for industry, and the helpful livable standard of American people. These are resourceful developments that have helped improve navigational air travel, satellites for weather, logical telecommunication, and other issues like the good, and occasional bad of the internet. Also this vitally includes laboratories to study, and help develop resourceful products within jet propulsion, air and water navigation, evaluating pollution, robotics, and "earth to orbit" gravitation. These are values since the Barack Obama presidential administration which included conflicting administrative decisions that have partly changed the atmosphere of some American technology. With this understanding of resourceful people whom have a strong background of technological skills, these people will be put on hold from their practice of scientific and engineering values that keeps America with advanced technology.

Observing the atmosphere of American technology the United States, and its government should try hard not to fall behind on NASA disciplines of technology. These become corporate and government business values which will make the American society weaker, or a vulnerable nation. If the American society does not advance in these values of technology this can be critical concerning other conflicting nations (c/o a few Americans) that have, and may continue to abuse the U.S. Constitutional establishment of rights. Even as the "U.S. Courts and Executive Orders" may need to intervene, the United States may become the victimized subject of other harmful or enemy nations. Then this is the understanding that these nations or "ourselves" can destroy the productive conditions of America as a well-developed society with future potential.

The United States Constitution becomes vital to various conditions of new and old technology. As each state government in America has a Constitution a vast amount of technological studies, and business activities became good, bad, and or conflicting within the existence of certain laws. Some conditions of this technology like "Drones, Tasers, Satellites, most Leasers" and other technology have certain restrictions, or they must be used under authorized professional, or reliable supervision. This is valuable to the concern that the most critical levels of professional or government authorized use of these product disciplines, and safety are lawfully, and U.S. Constitutionally applied for the American innocence of people.

On some occasions the U.S. government holds a close concern on what products, and technology can be sold to which foreign countries. These are usually defense related items such as military drones, nuclear technology and or weapons which the American system of government, and other international allies consider are dangerous, and or conflicting to National Security. Recently this has been observed with North Korea, Iran, and Libya whom fall into the category of countries that have conflicting issues of potential danger with certain technology. Iran has also captured a U.S. military drone, and along with North Korea both are potentially making an effort to create long range nuclear missiles.

There is and was the danger from Libya's former dictator Muammar Gaddafi who made his country dangerous for some American government officials, oil companies with contractors, and his own citizens. This was due to him commanding the Libyan army to kill their own citizens that disagreed with Muammar Gaddafi's, unethical ways of being a leader in their system of government. Also this, led to the 2nd serious attack on Libya by the United States government over the last two decades. Considering the most recent peace keeping attacks in 2011 it consisted of the U.S. military, and its allies (c/o England) executing military drone strikes that killed over 2,000 people of mostly an enemy capacity. This technology was providing precision bombing on at least 1,200 targets in Afghanistan, and Libya. Upon this understanding the United States, and the United Nations dose not try to monopolize dictatorship power, but they do enforce peace keeping missions of discipline, and humanity worldwide.

Another problem in Libya as it applies to corporate America consisted of a slowdown in oil exploration and production activities from companies such as ExxonMobil Corp, and ConocoPhillips Corp who's employees had to leave Libya for their own safety. These American oil companies earn billions of dollars a year with oil, and gas reserves from these international commodities of resourceful oil industry values. ConocoPhillips Corporation with their CEO James Mulva operates in more than 30 countries. Therefore ExxonMobil Corporation being the largest oil company in America and the world have a capacity of production levels that is an astute format of discipline. Observing the valued business operation of ConocoPhillips Corporation, and them being the 3rd largest oil and gas company in America have shown competitive issues of prosperity.

The ExxonMobil Corporation with their CEO Rex Tillerson has been operating in 45 countries which helps them create a vast amount of petroleum products. Then doing business not only in America, but worldwide becomes partly a careful review of research on National Security issues, geology and the oil industry internationally. Considering there is a vast amount of other duties such as operating and managing refineries, manufacturing, distribution, sales, and other important details ExxonMobil with other U.S. oil and gas company activities continue to keep U.S., and international laws within the boundary of their business.

Before the 1998 merger of Exxon and Mobil, the Exxon Valdez oil spill in 1989 was a geological disaster. After paying large fines Exxon Corp achieved record earnings with their CEO Lee Raymond, but the economy along with government had created restrictions that were observed within the Oil Pollution Act of 1990. Then by 2000, 2005, and 2010 the American oil industry slightly changed contrary to research, but also with numerous merger transactions, government legislative issues, and safety disciplines which recognized certain fatal accidents with Amoco Oil being a complex transition into BP. Contrary to these oil industry conflicts with logical research, and "National Security" reviews, America became an international issue that consisted of terror that caused a conflict to corporate businesses, the people, and the United States government.

As America with National Security concerns observes the September 11, 2001 attacks which was not prevented by any valued level of technology, the U.S. government, and or the people this tragedy stunned American citizens, and the world. This tragedy and disastrous attack with hijacked airplanes included the United States government, and some state governments being victimized with various corporations also suffering tremendous losses. United Airlines Inc, and American Airlines Inc loss people, various customers, and expensive airplanes during these 9-11 Report attacks. Following this tragedy the American market for air travel suffered certain economic hardships, and both companies became issues of corporate merger's which resulted in a "Corporate America" reduction of "four companies becoming two". This factor of issues means less businesses, in America have accumulated another economic conflict for the people, and various industry concerns. Understanding this, these were losses within the American society of people, tax revenue, and businesses which in the "coming future" was part of a severe economic change within the years to follow.

Some of these conflicts are part of the awareness to control or eliminate "international investments with international terrorism". With investments, and diversified National Security issues, some factors of the American society of government lacked issues of discipline to prevent these violent attacks against the United States.

These were internal issues of people throughout the American society that became complacent which included the George Bush administration, and various local government officials throughout America. Some other issues of complacent government and corporate business lead to a "banking and mortgage crisis" upon which some businesspeople with conflicting religious values even supported this crisis with confusion of an enemy foreign agenda. This enemy attack observing the 9-11 Report attacks has caused the 1st decade of 2000 "time of war" to be an expensive, and deadly conflict of war engagement for the United States in the Middle East.

The mortgage market in America during the 1990s up thru 2012 has been a massive "monopolized problem" only to be compared to the 1930s Great Depression. Instead of long lines at various banks which occurred during the 1929 stock market crash, now (c/o 2012 & 2013) people are moving on a month-by—month bases. They are living from house to house or within the resource of various apartments similar to "Tent Cities" in the 1930s. These millions of people are paying monthly rent until the house or apartment has ran into foreclosure, or any conflicting logical or reliable payments become conflicting apart from contract commitments or ownership. This economic recession of the 2000s has even included a severely high and unstable inflationary cost of gas, cigarettes, and other items to most all American consumers. Contrary to these factors some households survived this first decade of 2000 which has consisted of a housing market with record low rates of home ownership, record levels of inflation which includes gas and oil prices and a high rate of business failures.

The diversion of this economic crisis consist of the federal concern that some business operations whether they are large or small corporations including banks more than likely violated certain U.S. Anti-Trust laws. These are market dictating issues (c/o trust busting) within their control of various parts of the American real estate market which are vital economic issues. This is a factor that became a loss to numerous businesses, and entrepreneurs in an aggressive real estate expansion of architecture, engineering, and construction activity. Considering factual evidence this is observed in how the city of Chicago had over 50 overhead cranes working on new construction hi-rise buildings, and now their real estate market is over built (c/o 2010), and seriously under-funded.

Understanding these basic facts of an over built real estate market consist of now during 2012, and 2013 a conflict of conditions to restructure finances. This occurred with auctioning off properties with value due to the reasoning that they could not "sale or rent" these condominiums, exclusive office's, and or real estate fast enough to make a profit. Then with an American mortgage crisis, and one of the largest cities in America being over built, this will be a continuous reoccurring economic recession. Also this includes a troubled real estate, and banking market in America until millions of people regain economic value, and stability.

These issues with large losses applied to corporate and banking issues have a low rate of small business expansion's, and high unemployment. This has and will keep "the housing market" in conflicting shape. Then this also will consist of millions of people whom have lost their homes to an inappropriate market of factors including expensive law disputes in the courts. Then this will be a challenging credit review process within stable household earnings or purchases that will be a factor into the next decades to come.

Observing the American market of mortgage lending, bank lending, and issues during 2013 that are valuable to residential, and commercial properties has been part of a slightly positive correction from the 2007 recession. A full correction will take most all American regional business involvement to stabilize with productive market conditions. This is part of the fact that property within this capacity of "Land" issues are one of the few personal, government, and or business assets of occasional transactions that "cannot" be relocated "easily". Just as an address can exist in one place, or location (c/o a city, town, and or state) for hundreds of years as the business community, and society surrounding the property must be resourceful. Then they also must be detailed with involvement that is positive, and productive. Therefore this becomes an overall value which will be determined from the "local" logic of productive effort within regional citizens, business involvement, and government where property taxes must be logical.

The most productive monopolies, and or market controlling businesses in America have a value of paying property taxes, but lately some businesses and residents have had to argue to keep these tax rates low or fair to citizens. When individuals, families, small or large businesses including corporations pay taxes this condition of tax revenue appropriates a government budget to operate which is vital to future concerns. During 2007 an enormous amount of businesses, and banks failed with some filing bankruptcy, and this caused higher unemployment with a loss of government tax revenue. As this effected local governments more, the U.S. federal government was bailing out too "big or important too fail" businesses. Therefore the United States government money circulation is tremendously important which helped these large businesses with various franchise office's "temporally survive" throughout America.

Understanding some conflicting issues from the U.S. federal government certain cities with various businesses suffered in a variation of economic and social conditions of difficulty. Small business ownership between Northwest Indiana, and Northeast Illinois changed with numerous foreign people owning American businesses. This was a factor upon which a consolidation of American businesses, seem to close, and take tremendous losses to Middle Eastern new gas station owners who did not have to pay taxes for their first 7 years. These issues were part of an Endless Loop of tragic legal and social conflicts that potential and former American business owners suffered.

The next issue of concern became the factor that there was very few long term, or born in America owners of gas stations whom seem to survive this victimized resource of American economic times. Considering these issues a conditional observation occurred when American owned businesses in and near large cities became a conflict due to their good, bad, and conflicting ambition of expansion. Contrary to this, including terrorist attacks with expensive damage this also hit black American business owners, and automobile dealerships hard in various regions including the mid-west of the United States.

Considering the recent economic problems that America suffered, and endured an enormous resource of markets could not survive. To restructure a market within this level of business activity, most people would have to reestablish their work, and professional skills of disciplines for long term commitments. Then as these extensive or comparable occupational resources became vital to the U.S. Constitutional level of business existence that is acceptable in America most everyone's workload increased with conflicts. Therefore various markets, the creation of monopolies with patents, and other vital factors of prosperous business in America had taken a down fall which will be extensive to overcome in the future.

CHAPTER FIVE

The American Infrastructure Market

An American Study Of Business & Monopolies

The American Infrastructure Market

Observing the American infrastructure that has consist of a diversified market of businesses, and government values is part of a consolidation to move forward with upgrades which has been an occasional challenge. These are also regulatory, and contractual issues factored from the United States Department of Transportation, Energy, Labor, and even Defense which includes other government entities with appropriated state and federal funds. On occasions this includes the condition of appropriated funds that surround and support most all state and local governments when an infrastructure project is legislatively important and relevant. Also upon these factors, which includes governed legislative, and occasional judicial concerns that somewhat intervene with executive branch decision making, the subject of a better society will be established. This is mostly part of American professional engineering, construction, labor issues, and management which includes various businesses, and some monopolies.

Considering the first decade of 2000 the infrastructure of roads, highways, bridges, dams, storm water drainage, and wastewater sewer systems have been vital concerns in America. Observing this becomes a factual issue when an enormous amount of citizens have been injured by large sinkholes on and below certain roadways. This even included one man in Florida being engulfed into a sinkhole without his body being recovered. The victim Jeff Bush was sleeping in his room at his home when a large sinkhole overcame his ability to survive the sinking downward force. This occurred at his Seffner, Florida house which he shared with his brother, and a few other family members.

The tremendous amount of sinkholes in America is the cause, and issue of sub-grade hollow underground components washed away by water. This then forces the surface components to sink below grade levels of most foundations. Therefore from underground water in the sub-grade this becomes dangerous to all above ground components with added severe problems.

Sinkholes in roadways and other places are unexpected issues of dangerous parts of the infrastructure from mostly obsolete sewers, water utilities, and uncontained underground water. Water at this level is most times not visible. These are roadway and landscape conditions that can be tremendous in danger, and cause damage to any nearby land supported assets, and people in that vicinity. Then this includes the vital need for upgrades within feasibilities from government, and professional engineering firms with studies, and evaluated utility, or sub-grade water disciplines. Therefore various utility companies working close with government has been a critical concern in most regions of the United States which is a priority to correct this vital problem throughout a vast amount of American regions.

Public utilities, and Americas infrastructure within the changing times, and technology must apply to the United States Constitution as it concerns to the elimination of public health problems, and suffering. These valuable concerns consist of workable issues of legal disciplines, and government enforcement responsibilities for the people. The people of America also depend on an infrastructure that has been partly developed by companies like American Telephone & Telegraph Corporation, and a vast amount of electric utility companies that operate from the patents of Thomas Edison, Alexander Bell, and others. Then this also consisted of water and wastewater treatment plants with field operations which all are valued under the laws of the Constitution in all states, and the federal government with professional commissions.

Considering the legal format of technology in America has been an observation of Chief Justice John Roberts, and a few others they have legal questions with constitutional value that continue to be discussed. Contrary to that fact enough of these issues have not been argued in the courts. His occasional review of decisions by the U.S. Supreme Court, consist of how the Constitution, and certain laws apply to advanced technology. Then these issues of technology and the laws along with the Constitution sometimes include the infrastructure with responsible issues of lawful liability similar to U.S. Anti-Trust laws.

Another Justice member Clarence Thomas provided discussions which becomes how the 4th Amendment can apply to a computer hard drive observing the privacy rights of that memory as stored information. The Rights of Privacy on a computer's hard drive could apply to the use of cell phone towers, and satellites contrary to a stolen computer or the invaded privacy of hacking a computer or a cell phones memory, and or database. Contrary to the Federal Communication Commission's regulatory establishment of laws,

Americas resources of infrastructure values is still based on public utility, public health, and public policy conditions of heavily well belt structures.

Understanding the advancement of American roads, bridges, and other needed projects (c/o the 1st decade of 2000) is factual that they are usually part of a regions safety, economic, and cost of living standards. Contrary to these facts the process of infrastructure upgrading projects must be done without fatal accidents. The Minnesota 2007 bridge collapse was one of the worse in decades, which was slightly different from the 1982 Cline Avenue bridge collapse of northwest Indiana. This Minnesota construction upgrading contract had a cost of $5.2 million dollars for Hurcon Incorporated, upon which 13 people were killed and 145 others were injured. Additional cost for reconstruction and design of the Minnesota bridge started at $50 million to a final cost of around $250 million dollars which most all was completed by September of 2008 the next year. The Cline Bridges cost $250 million dollars in 1982, but at least 15 construction workers were killed during the collapse with the bridge being completed in 1986.

Both Indiana and Minnesota bridge accidents were under construction to advance or upgrade the highway travel system throughout these regions of America. Then considering these important projects that are a careful discipline of government with engineering, and construction these are vital issues within resourceful developments of the infrastructure. Contrary to these accidents there has been billions of dollars spent on other American bridge projects of this magnitude that where completed without severe problems. Therefore considering most professional values the input of the local people is vital, and or appropriate with logical opinions. Then these opinions must be reviewed considering that they are occasionally argued in a hearing applicable to the laws of the individual states, and the United States government. This is the format of regulated disciplines for the citizens to be heard, and their needs understood.

All infrastructure necessities with detailed business and financial conditional standards are part of important government tax revenue managing values. This becomes the indifference of public utility company funded projects with business service activities. Some of these utility company projects and continuous upgrades have used the same "Engineering firms" for close to 100 years. Observing these facts most all projects become important within keeping up to date utility service equipment connected to the infrastructure. Even after various storms that have caused massive damage, and blackouts the repair of utility systems is vital. Therefore this becomes the utility company work of having to put water, communications, and more so electricity back on line for capacity usage, and electrical output throughout regional systems.

Every city, and state in America consist of public utility monopolies along with infrastructure values that must be updated, or some service details of the infrastructure will fail to be workable. This valuable issue which can be a problem to the American general public, businesses, and even government requires various industries, and government to work together on issues with good decisions. Then during the government tenure of U.S. Energy Department Secretary Spencer Abraham this was a factor during the 2003 electrical blackout. This affected 55 million citizens, and caused $6 billion dollars in damage in the United States, and a certain amount of parts of Canada.

Observing this reoccurring issue (c/o electrical blackouts) as a technical problem, and professional level of evaluations, the utility companies stay prepared to correct any similar problems. This becomes vital, but the company FirstEnergy as a, electric utility had a large base of liquidity. Understanding this is common in some large utility companies the indifference within facts is that they failed to compensate liability standards which lead to this 2003 electric utility incident.

The 2003 east coast electrical blackout was a multi-billion dollar issue. FirstEnergy being the company at fault took 3 days to correct this blackout of electricity that was not the cause of commonly known bad weather. This also is a factor of why public utility companies generate, and manage enormous amounts of income for contingent liability operating expenses. Therefore as liquidity is managed for various reasons, and then they must put cash liquidity into good investments with operating expenses, these become details of their monopolized existence and liability in business. Then their business operation of public monopolized trust has appropriate liability.

Mother-nature and various weather conditions throughout the many geological regions of America are some of the most demanding challenges that the people of America live with concerning a productive and workable infrastructure. From Joplin, Missouri to places such as New Jersey, New York City, New Orleans, and other cities and regions affected from weather related damages during the 1st decade and a half of 2000 have been tremendous. This has been observed and factored within the aging infrastructure of utilities that provide services to most all commercial and residential facilities. Then more so this applies to obsolete storm water utility components that could not compensate the storm-serge of hurricane Katrina (2005), hurricane Ike (2008), tornados in Joplin, Missouri, and various storm activities in parts of Texas during 2012.

Considering tropical storm Sandy in the northeastern part of America during 2013 following certain flooding in 2011 and 2012 has been devastating to those citizens, and their property. Some parts of New Jersey (c/o Newark, Jersey Shores & others) have been hit over and over lately with extensive flooding and wind damage. The tremendous effect to Jersey Shores includes the storm-serge from tropical storm Sandy which has left severe regional damage. As of February 2013 hurricane Sandy becoming a tropical storm has caused damages estimated at $63 billion dollars compared to hurricane Katrina at $108 billion dollars with both storms leaving citizens slightly homeless.

Almost 65% of the hurricane damages within cost include most everything except certain parts of the infrastructure. Observing hurricane Katrina the infrastructure failure was the" worse" part of the tremendous damage that occurred. This was due to the fact that Mayor Ray Nagan and others did not recognize or consider the importance of upgrading the levees dividing New Orleans from the waters of Lake Pontchartrain, and the Gulf of Mexico. Other damages included trees, wildlife, boats, cars, commercial, and residential properties along with public utility equipment. Therefore hurricane Katrina with damages at $108 billion dollars the levees to control water from the Gulf of Mexico where some of the most vital issues of repairs, and upgrades. This was one of the most vital infrastructure concerns to be completed before New Orleans, and that southern region of America could go forward with a revitalized levee system.

As it applies to public land, and waterways the last few U.S. Department of Interior Secretaries to observe was Bruce Babbitt,

Gale Norton, Dirk Kempthorme, Lynn Scarlett, and Ken Salizar who's office has vital duties for the American infrastructure. These U.S. government duties consist of managing public lands, various projects, national forest preserves, and mapping. Observing various American values these people, and their office become important in locating bridges, levees, dams, rivers, oceans, highways, and other important structures with public land. Therefore when this includes details that should be recognized geographically on maps, certain evaluations by others in government (c/o public or private land service professionals) there has been a lack of appropriations that keep the people, and their assets protected, or safe.

Contrary to President's Bill Clinton, George Bush, and Barack Obama the U.S. Department of Interior having a good workable relationship with the U.S. Departments of Transportation, Energy and others like the Bureau of Reclamation have been vital for productive levels of effectiveness. The U.S. Secretary of Transportation Ray LaHood during February of 2013 has been extremely concerned with others about federal budget cuts. These budgets cuts (c/o sequestration) could slow down some infrastructure projects, and affect air traffic controlled travel at major U.S. airports throughout the United States. This becomes the challenge within the format to improve the infrastructure to keep effectively safe highway, and air travel astute which helps the economy from extensive damages, or harmful diversions. Therefore with other issues apart from the infrastructure, if some monopolized public utilities along with government utilities were going to be productive these departments of government must be responsible, and effective. Then this is the consideration that they should have had a better workable process of discipline, and financial management.

During the tenure of Bruce Babbitt as the Governor of Arizona in the 1980s his experience with Arizona Public Service Company, and the infrastructure consisted of valued issues of expansion. This was during the last years of President Ronald Reagan's time, and tenure in office, and during a population expansion in Arizona that occurred with resourceful engineering, and new construction. Also this included companies like General Electric Corporation with Jack Welch the CEO who took manufacturing, and selling electrical transformers to new heights. Then this became the understanding of how the best resources of public utility equipment, and the infrastructure became compatible and workable for the citizens, the people, and even businesses achieving logical stability and growth. Recently this level of new construction expansion has been unprofitable, and this has been part of the mortgage, and overall debt crisis leading up to 2013.

The transition of new household subdivisions in the Phoenix metropolitan area for Arizona Public Service Company, General Electric Corporation, and a few other professional businesses was creating a time of economic prosperity. This was the tremendous growth within activities throughout metropolitan Phoenix, Arizona which included various cities, towns, and even Mesa, Arizona that increased its population by over 100,000 people during the mid to late 1980s. Understanding this level of populated growth became an issue for a need of additional infrastructure, housing, and utilities.

Considering this strong money circulation in Arizona that occurred with infrastructure upgrades that would last for decades, this long term investment was valuable. This value included whether the economy was in good or bad shape, but most of these projects had certain government and prosperous values of business expansion. Then the worse part of these factors included how years later various business owners were held back, which was due to an increase in crime. Therefore business owners and more so citizens were victimized by other Americans, and some issues of Mexican immigrants transporting drugs similar to "Middle East" terrorists with conflicting opinions occasionally supported by various bad Americans.

Upon a comparison of infrastructure and public utilities between Phoenix, and New York City a large difference of competitive utility values has been consistent upon how more gas or electricity is provided by regional utility companies. This has been a vital working process which the city Engineering Departments of Phoenix is observing more electricity, and New York City has a concern of observing more natural gas in the infrastructure. Observing these two different regions of weather and climate conditions, New York City has suffered from more gas and electrical transformer explosions due to its good, bad, and more so slightly obsolete sub-grade utilities.

Considering the hotter temperatures in the Phoenix metropolitan area their region has consisted of less explosions, and blackouts. New York and Chicago have been fairly kwon in their regional activity for these temporary blackout issues. Then these conflicts which have occurred due to more electricity than gas as it applies to public utilities are regulated due to the temperature. These are important resources in this state capital city of Phoenix, Arizona as well other states. Then this understanding has been more sustainable to the weather conditions that affect the infrastructure.

To understand the capacity of business monopoly, and infrastructure values within the telecommunication industry various companies such as American Telephone & Telegraph Corporation (AT&T) has managed their overall system with cliental in every city, and state. Their level of competition has been different throughout these many regions of America, but they hold a logical and extensive level of patent rights. These patent rights are important to most of the equipment that is installed in the sub-grade, and most elevated parts of the infrastructure.

Considering the telecommunication infrastructure there are utility poles, and towers throughout the American societies infrastructure that are part of a valuable market. A vast majority of this equipment is patented by AT&T Corporation, various utility companies, and what use to be General Telephone & Electronics Corporation (GTE) whom now is Verizon Wireless Communications. Verizon is a corporation operating mostly on the east coast, but with a strong presence in most other states. This is their understanding of heavily investing in communication mergers, and acquisitions which includes some values of the U.S. infrastructure since the beginning of 2000. Then they have had a discipline to create, and manage the 2nd largest (c/o 2013) U.S. wireless and some wired communication services. Therefore this has made them a productive part of the changing times within communication technology.

The observed factor of AT&T Corporation having a level of controlled ownership of communication equipment in the American infrastructure has been a challenging factor with the U.S. government, and other communication companies. This also consisted of Sprint Corporation during the 1980s installing fiber optic communication cables throughout various parts of the United States. Considering this occurred during a very competitive market between these corporate businesses, this was considered a competitive and most times lawfully conditional business investment of value. These two companies caused part of the establishment of U.S. Anti-Trust laws to be constantly evaluated. This became formal within the markets of creating a local telephone company option with a long distance telephone company option to all American telecommunication consumers.

Understanding various parts of the federal laws with patents these assets and employees that AT&T Corporation uses to keep their monopolized utility system almost second to none is maintained with a level of market control and discipline. Then this is the format of how they have invested in their telecommunication business to the extent that they service their equipment in residential and commercial facilities throughout all parts of the United States. This vitally includes most all conditions of underground, and higher elevated telephone poles, and towers supporting the utility infrastructure of telecommunication cables and equipment. Therefore this is considered an effective business plan in America, and throughout the world that is productive.

Verizon Communication Inc has made business investments throughout the American infrastructure which over the years of the late 1990s as Bell Atlantic (c/o some AT&T rights) up until 2000 has consisted of the erecting of a massive amount of cell phone towers. This expensive resource of business utility upgrades by Verizon with their current CEO Lowell McAdam is part of the asset expansion values from mergers, and buyouts which they acquired from Bell Atlantic, and other equipment from the buyout of GTE. The former CEO & Chairman Raymond Smith of Bell Atlantic, and NYNEX with their CEO Ivan Seidenberg in 1996 shared these telecommunication CEO duties upon becoming Verizon, with market changing expansion issues.

Contrary to Verizon buying; the former WorldCom assets they also moved their headquarters from Philadelphia to New York City. This existed before establishing the name Verizon Incorporated, in 2000 as this negotiated issue of corporate discipline continued to become more, and more astute within logical business values. Therefore their resourceful priorities to work together had become astute with wireless telecommunication, and most times with effective outcomes.

As the infrastructure of telecommunication equipment and operating systems of advanced technology changed with the times, the internet became a strong component within wireless, and wired communication connections. The internet being the established component of telephone modems has made advancements in the use of computers being connected to each other an increasing level of access. This is the format of how they are connected to households, corporations, and even the government's massive computer "server and data" base systems.

These systems at IBM, Microsoft, Apple, General Electric, all utilities companies, all levels of American government, and others consist of factors of technology that have made extreme adjustments. These various corporations and government make adjustments to the American society we live in with regulated standards. These standards of regulation consist of the numerous changing ways to conduct a vast amount of business transactions in America.

One changing market example is during the first decade of 2000, millions of Americans, and people from other countries became more dependent on the adjustment of paying their monthly bills through the internet. Considering this factor there are millions of Americans that buy less stamps from the U.S. Post Office. Then the U.S. Postal Service has taken severe financial losses from this transitional process of technology, and other issues of economic oversight. Therefore eliminating an extreme amount of U.S. Postal Service resources that have been considered excessive cost has become a priority.

The clear conditional establishment of the internet has become a tremendous service in America, and other countries with good, and some bad values of liability. Observing the foundation of business in American corporations, and some small business expansions the internet has connected businesses, and customers in a global capacity, but this also includes a level of occasional fraud that is complex to control. Understanding this, most major corporate businesses are still conditionally safe for consumers with responsible values of liability. Contrary to this resource of commerce through the infrastructure of information technology advancements the consolidation of lawful economic disciplines are still being reviewed carefully.

After tremendous expansion of the internet even pirating, and bootlegging of movies, and music has become a multibillion dollar illegal business issue for the courts. These are downloaded music, and movie products from the internet, and then sold illegally in various parts of the American society. This illegal concept of business takes away from the original royalties for people that made this level of effort in business, art, or entertainment famous, or productive. A major economic loss is also observed in the lawful wholesale, and retail store sales activity of these items. Therefore this is similar to an author, musician, or inventor's exclusive rights from their workable developments.

As critical infrastructure issues advance, but Americas economic conditions are partly troublesome this becomes part of an overall issue of business, and government restructuring. These levels of restructuring are important to a vast amount of business valued existence in the United States, and throughout various parts of the world. Observing these issues of restructuring government and some monopolizing corporations with various budget issues for the internet's infrastructure are valuable, but other critical parts of the U.S. infrastructure like managing satellites, and storm water can't be forgotten, or ignored. Then therefore the more new technology, the more work and evaluations become vital with regulation.

Contrary to new aged issues within information technology, an older resource of industry with technological values have been constantly evaluated, and upgraded with the infrastructure system of railroads, and other transportation issues in America. For the last two centuries upgrading the American infrastructure of railroad tracks, and equipment have been a business, and government transportation priority. With more advanced locomotive trains made by General Electric Corporation, and General Motors Corporation for Norfolk Southern, Union Pacific Corporation (UP), Burlington Northern and Santa Fe Railway (BNSF), and other railroad companies this industry has kept up with the changing times.

The changing times, becomes an improved upgrade of railroad shipping, and passenger travel business disciplines. This even includes most subway passenger trains in various large cities upon which logical upgrades are vital for safety, efficiency to perform, and newer standards of compatibility. The system of passenger and freight train services, and manufacturing have kept design, engineering, and construction operations busy with logical engineering, and government disciplines to improve, and maintain manufacturing standards, and government regulatory importance.

Norfolk Southern Railway, and various railroad systems like those used in city subway systems that operate 24 hours a day, and 7 days a week require continuous maintenance, repairs, and upgrades of operating equipment. These business, and infrastructure details at Norfolk Southern Railway, includes their company managing, and operating resources of 20,000 route miles in 22 states. This also includes other staging, fueling properties, and railroad shipping yards in a variety of appropriate states.

Norfolk Southern has monopoly values of control on Americas east coast, and certain parts of the Midwest of the United States which intervenes with other diversified train systems, and services. This includes the massive New York City, Chicago, Los Angeles, Dallas, and other subway systems including the activity of the National Railroad Passenger Corporation which is "Amtrak". These are the managing disciplines of control that the Norfolk Southern CEO Charles Moorman has managed, and how the company has to coordinate their work within thousands of miles of railroad business values. Also this is vital to maintain their market throughout the Eastern railroad system which includes Amtrak that is applicable to the United States and other American routes which even includes Ontario, Canada.

Observing the American west coast region, certain parts of the Midwest and various southern states throughout the United States consist of protected railroad routes for the Burlington Northern and Santa Fe Railroad. They also are conditional competitors with the largest railroad network operated by Union Pacific Railroad. The level of Union Pacific Railroad freight and passenger service operates within 31,900 miles of routed tracks (c/o 2012) with 44,000 employees with their Chairman James Young, and CEO Jack Koraleski. Burlington Northern and Santa Fe Railway with their CEO Matthew Rose operates on 32,166 miles of railroad which are similar regional routes to Union Pacific. Burlington Northern and Santa Fe Railroad which is a wholly owned subsidiary of Berkshire Hathaway Inc. gives, them an additional base of liquidity. Therefore with various railroad business concerns the United States Department of Transportation, and all state governments maintain their awareness of these transportation values with support and government regulatory appropriations.

The monopolized resource of businesses that control large parts or percentages of these national markets are usually helpful to other small and large businesses. As it applies to railroad services in America the Federal Railroad Administration is authorized by the U.S. Department of Transportation to keep lawful operations safe, and effective for the general public. The Federal Aviation Administration, the U.S. Department of Energy, and a few others such as within agriculture, communications, and reclamation have been known to deal with massive markets, and the infrastructure. Therefore with public, private research which includes businesses, the citizens, and government working together can make progress during the future within changing times of industry.

CHAPTER SIX

Public Monopolies & The U.S. System Of Government

An American Study Of Business & Monopolies

Public Monopolies & The U.S. System Of Government

Public monopolies leading up to the 1st decade of 2000 in the United States have existed with various resources of industry which includes the changing times, and a conflicting American economy. Some of these industries include public housing, government owned toll roads, harbors, railroads, airports, the United States Postal Service, and various wastewater and water treatment plants. Another resource includes communications, natural gas and electric utilities, which is indifferent with the U.S. government also managing a resource of government sponsored enterprises. Upon these industry values whether public, private, or government businesses it's still important that these resources of business earn a logical and financially sound profit (c/o tax revenue) without any disastrous conflicts of liability.

Understanding monopolies, the U.S. government is a controlling partner in a variation of businesses, and organizations which is a value of appropriate enterprise resources with Constitutional issues of domestic tranquility. Contrary to these factors with Constitutional Law considerations of resource, the U.S. Post Office with Postmaster General Patrick Donahoe being part of obvious public monopolies is a similar economic concern to the good, and bad financial matters of Amtrak railroad services.

Even the bailout of American International Group (AIG) during the tenure of their CEO Maurice Greenberg can be observed as another failing business that monopolized in various ways, and then needed financial help, form the U.S. government. Then considering AIG, the United States Postal Service (est. 1770), Amtrak, and a few others with involvement in these business and government transitions leaves, "one" vital question remaining. That question is "will the U.S. system of government continue" to have problems in the future control, or consideration of bailing out other corporate business operations?

AIG had been providing certain types of insurance products which included insuring various financial investments, and other insurance products with responsible services. This had been maintained with good, and logical presence in American business until their part of the 2007 financial crisis occurred. During that same time the U.S. Postal

Service, and others suffered also, but Amtrak's business economic problems started decades before 1970.

The issue that Amtrak with their CEO and President Joseph Boardman had endured was financially an issue during 2012. This was similar to a few other railroad companies that the U.S. government controls, observes, and closely regulates. These are corporate businesses that no matter how bad they may have violated the law or did not consist of efficient management the U.S. federal government considered a bailout of their extreme problems or insecurity. Then this led us as Americans to compare a variation of public monopolized businesses that closely work, and depend on support from the United States government. Therefore these massive monopolized business operations had to be restructured by the United States government instead of being operated in a profitable concept of public, and or private level of concern within business ownership with the exception of AIG, and a few others.

The U.S. Post Office over centuries has been doing business with every household, business, and organization in America with discipline, but this did not guarantee their best level of earnings which is based on occasional tax revenue. As these businesses were failing in 2005 the U.S. government temporarily took ownership of AIG to save this large insurance company. Now (c/o 2012) the U.S. government is restructuring the United States Postal Service which is part of the good and bad resources of a public monopoly. These are some of the same disciplines of business that Amtrak (c/o the National Railroad Passenger Corporation) endured during the 1960s, and 1970s with their restructured business plan that included the U.S. government. This is partly because Amtrak operates in 46 American states making it too big to fail, and now they are a non-profit corporation that is financially supported by the United States government, and the Congress.

As to what is closely considered a monopoly or non-for-profit corporate business that provides various services, another government resource consist of providing certain emergency relief products, and other concerns that are important to the people. This even includes a government process of managing certain health care facilities which is funded through government tax revenue values. Then various Medicade and or Medicare programs and public housing is part of providing people with important conditional services that are vital.

The objective of tax revenue funded services from the state or the U.S. federal government has become a budget argument between Republicans, Democrats, and some independents in most all parts of government. Therefore during 2013 this has been part of the sequestration budget cuts from various U.S. government services that has caused a level of conflicting grief.

Considering the American society of various people that have observed an issue of sequestration, housing has been one of the lower level issues of discussion, but it is still a vital part of the present recession. Then this issue apart from cutting the spending on public housing is at a level of historical concern with the U.S. Department of Housing and Urban Development, and the United States government that observes this crisis. The issue of public housing is another major public monopoly concern within the format of the U.S. government having various business enterprise resources that goes back as far as the Great Depression. Those years of the 1930s consisted of "tent cities", all over America with people that had no home to live inn. Therefore the economic crisis of the 1st decade of 2000 became similar to those hard financial times in America.

Observing American publicly traded corporations various stocks and bonds are a valid resource of American economic prosperity outside of 1929, and now 2007. This is also a good and bad evaluation of how corporate stocks and bonds have ownership values that the American general public is offered to participate in with the regulatory values of the Securities and Exchange Commission. As the Securities and Exchange Commission consist of an enormous amount of corporations (c/o some monopolies), and investors they have dealt with Enron, WorldCom, and some health care providers like HealthSouth. Understanding this, the people, government, and some businesses were victimized. Contrary to better corporate investments these are just a few issues that have occasionally hit the American economy hard with bad decisions from big business.

Even though HealthSouth has still been considered a prosperous health care business that suffered a scandal, they still operate in 28 states with 60,000 employees. This has been another era of problems that became an overall market controlling business issue of concern with Enron, and WorldCom as America's economy suffered tremendous losses which had to be restructured. Unlike HealthSouth who is still in business, the concept of Enron, and WorldCom assets have been seized, and sold off with other business components dissolved. These monopoly controlling issues have been partly the cause of an American recession of severe ignorance, and or confusion. Therefore the 1st few decades of 2000 will be tremendous throughout the American society with numerous businesses restructuring if logical efforts are considered properly.

During the year of 2007 America conditionally became a witness to various victims of a residential, commercial, and investment banking industry that had eluded certain small investors, and normal consumers. Then various people (c/o government & big business) engaged in an expanding financial sector of businesses that conditionally became an issue that was considered financially too big to "fail", or maybe to big "manage". As these financial institutions suffered problems this hurts the overall American economy from small business growth with some U.S. Anti-Trust laws, and with Constitutional laws being ignored. Understanding this, these private companies, and some professional offices that work with government, and even utility companies had a duty, and need to restructure "if possible" with their logical business values.

Another factor within a financial crisis includes the public business sectors along with the American system of government. This was a concern like at wastewater, and water treatment plants which are vital operations usually funded by service fees, local government, and financial investments with underwritten bonds. Most of these bonds are offered through government auctions, but lately some municipal bonds like in Chicago as one of the larger markets has lately been rated lower, and graded as not a secured investment.

Contrary to the fact of monopolized control within various markets the state governments with the United States Constitution and government have always become vital law that observes professional engineering issues. This is observed after sewers failed with sinkholes, and numerous other severe floods occurred during an economic crisis. Understanding this, these are issues to argue in the courts to regain American equity on a social, professional, and business level of equality with resources of discipline.

Hundreds of millions of people, households, churches, organizations, businesses, and government in America everyday have engagements with various public utility companies which they depend on with various monopolized services. Tennessee Valley Authority (TVA) is the largest government owned "electric" public utility monopoly in the United States. As TVA, is observed throughout the U.S. Department of Energy numerous changes, and upgrades to the electrical grid have been most times a responsible course of professional engineering, and technology. Therefore logical electric public utility service issues with agreements have been appropriately provided to a massive amount of citizens.

Contrary to TVA some utility values are also part of government regulated issues, and technological values within the distribution of electricity as valued with industry standards. These are values upon which has been part of the integrating of SCADA control systems. This provides electrical and computer monitoring system controls, and details out problems in the overall utility distribution and operating process and system. Then these are factors that have kept these industry values productive, and consisting of conflicting or controlling cost with operating issues for their consumers.

Safety and clean energy during the first decade of 2000 have consisted of issues supported by various electrical power distribution industry standards. Also this includes some energy policy values from the U.S. Presidencies of George Bush, and Barack Obama with the observation of other presidential values. Today (observing 2010) the largest conflicts of clean energy is observed within oil companies, coal fired energy power plants, and a few other issues of chemical pollution in the United States. Also as major "Energy Legislative" factors have been considered, a diversified resource of systems, have been created. This includes renewable solar energy, wind power energy generating equipment, and throughout most facilities the establishing of low energy light bulbs with other government option energy conservation values.

Another concept of government and industry has been the factual concern of U.S. Energy, and Environmental Protection regulated issues that are important for various business conditions to be safe, and effective. These are important parts of the infrastructure, and the environment surrounding these industries, and businesses that are too vital to ignore, and too much of a necessity for productive use by the American society of people. Even the importance of oil or chemical spills on land, and more so in rivers, lakes, and ocean waterways have been a tremendous problem along with chemical explosions that contaminate the air, and land. The Texas City, Texas BP (formerly Amoco Oil) fatal explosion in 2005 was a conditional concern in this same energy, and environmental factor of American industry. Considering these are important technology values with some new chemical processes, and values that have been reviewed with appropriate concern this factor of the changing times must be part of lawful, and updated reviews.

Some newer energy concerns, includes "the Clean Energy Act" of 2005. These legislative issues consist of numerous disciplines of energy standards including coal fired energy, hydroelectric energy, clean energy nuclear powered plants, and now renewable energy sources like solar, and wind powered energy. Some of these resources are part of conditional issues of fossil fuels which is a delicate process of coal or other ground materials being burned as an energy resource of technology. This resource of fossil fuel technology on occasions will take time with innovation, and certain evaluations for a better consolidation of development.

The concentration of fossil fuels and various nuclear energy developments along with coal are conditional resources of technology where high temperatures are used to melt compounds of natural commodities to produce energy. Then nuclear energy contrary to coal can be environmentally worse, but the cost to safely renovate, and or upgrade American electric utility plants with nuclear energy have been considered too expensive. These are the resourceful types of energy plants in operation at TVA that are providing electricity for Tennessee, parts of Alabama, Mississippi, and Kentucky with some small portions of Georgia, North Carolina, and Virginia managed. This massive resource of "Energy", consist of a vast amount of good conditions, but on occasions it has been considered a public health concern if responsible engineering disciplines are not applied.

As a public monopoly Tennessee Valley Authority and businesses such as various Edison companies have been part of electric utility engineering, and government regulation for decades. These, and other utility companies owned by any factor of government have worked to somewhat keep market control astute, and valued. America's resource of engineering values within students, and professionals have been considered a losing factor with not enough engineering graduates, or supportive people advancing in this profession, and occupation with value. Observing this, engineering is one factor about Enron controlling a public utility as in electrical power included the concept of electrical engineering professionals (c/o the financial markets) whom took a large unprofessional loss.

A discretionary business resource can be observed similar to the issues of a financial company owning an engineering firm acting under investment bank guidelines as a public monopoly. Investment Banking and Professional Engineering are two separate professions of different vital disciplines which are most times closely regulated by various entities of the U.S. system of government. Therefore Enron with their CEO Ken Lay appropriated a different level of losses compared to some TVA activities, and Edison company franchises which have provided lawfully high standards in this industry.

Contrary to the advancements of TVA and numerous Edison companies that have achieved mechanical, civil, chemical, and electrical engineering developments. These are part of the consolidated developments of nuclear energy that have more so become a value in America's fleet of U.S. Department of Defense battleships. Understanding the transition between coal, gas, diesel fuel, and now nuclear energy becoming effective for large ships, and submarines that are sailing on, and under American, and international waters is the containment values of this technology. Considering these factors which include government building new U.S. Navy vessels to operate from nuclear energy is an advancement, but constructing more electric utility plants with nuclear technology on line as a utility is another expensive challenge.

As Edison electric franchises such as Commonwealth Edison (ComEd of Chicago), Consolidated Edison (ConEd of New York City), Detroit Edison (DTE), and Southern California Edison they observe the concept of nuclear energy as technology which is valued with cautionary responsibilities in large cities. Considering ComEd of Chicago, and Northern Illinois they provide electric and gas services to 3.7 million customers (c/o 2012) with similar others like ConEd of New York City, and a few other utilities serving large populations. California is geographically the most conflicting for nuclear energy due to numerous earthquakes, except for a couple reactors and test sites between desert plans near, and in Arizona. These large cities with enormous populations could be threatened with life time contamination, and radioactive deaths, or injuries if nuclear energy was their main source of electricity, and a bad accident occurs. Then this therefore can be observed as the small or large utility value within the input, and output of utilities with profit margins. These issues are listed within their bookkeeping standards, and their public safety values.

One of Americans largest nuclear facility accidents was the Three Mile Island incident which nuclear chemicals spilled out of a reactor. This Three Mile Island Plant and project in Dauphin County, Pennsylvania consisted of a non-fatal accident in 1978 which took careful cleanup for 16 years, and had a cost of $1 billion dollars. The U.S. Nuclear Regulatory Commission determined that this 1978 accident was serious, but it was not a tremendous concern for the evacuation of nearby citizens, or continuous alarm. Then similar to other utility plants throughout America, these factors began to become more efficient and safe which consisted of a vast amount of changes. These where relevant industry standard changes which had to be made professionally, including at this remote Three Mile Island operation which is an enormous nuclear power plant, and a continuous engineering and construction project site.

Before the establishment of FirstEnergy Corporation, General Public Utilities, and Metropolitan Edison owned, and operated the Three Mile Island nuclear energy plant. Their present 2013 CEO & President Anthony Alexander has held his post since 2007 in these combined companies, which was four years after FirstEnergy was partly at fault for the 2003 northeast blackout. This was part of a "Endless Loop Crisis" of electrical public utility companies that had established complacent problems, and loss some understanding of productive people working together in this vital industry.

Another issue that accumulated from a buyout/merger of Metropolitan Edison is that the Pennsylvania Public Utility Commission decided to investigate the former company because of a lack of workable utility standards. Then this commission had observation that their service reliability had fallen below professional standards which became a utility, and citizen issue of vital concern. The governor Ted Strickland of Ohio which is where FirstEnergy's headquarters is located in Akron, Ohio was well pleased with their decision to purchase the rights, and develop a compressed-air electric generating plant in Norton, Ohio. Contrary to this being one of the largest and most innovated compressed-air plants in the world, these are a few of the good and bad efforts within issues that FirstEnergy, and other electric utility companies established as a professional challenge.

There are other nuclear energy plants and reactors in a few states near various other major cities which they all are heavily regulated by the United States Nuclear Regulatory Commission with their 2012 Chairman Allison Macfarlane to keep this technology hopefully astute. Understanding the U.S. Department of Energy was established in 1977 with former U.S. President Jimmy Carter the duty of regulating all forms of energy with policy disciplines that apply to different states also consist of different conditions. These are different geographical regions that use or produce electric energy in a few diversified ways including developments under U.S. Nuclear Regulatory Commission matters, and their jurisdictions. Some nuclear energy studies and research are conducted at facilities like Oak Ridge National Laboratory in Tennessee which is managed for the United States Department of Energy to improve engineering, design, and scientific-principals.

The Nuclear Regulatory Commission with the U.S. Department of Energy becomes the concept of utility business matters in places outside of Chicago, Detroit, and New York City. Also this includes other east coast locations, but not many parts of California due to earthquakes, although Arizona had numerous test sites, and nuclear waste storage resource concerns. Then cities like Dallas, Texas and parts of a few other southern states which most of these places are usually hubs for research and development have consisted of advancements on how technology effect society. This is due to their heavy state, and federal government presence of regulatory duties. Therefore the amount of money spent on engineering design, building trades, nuclear energy research, and managing maintenance for these facilities to stay in compliance can be tremendous which includes conflicting occasional public opinions.

Considering public monopoly concerns within utility companies, one of the biggest, and most massive government owned monopoly groups of enterprises consist of every city, town, county, and or occasionally state owned "Wastewater Sanitary facility or District". This also most times includes a "Storm Water Management District" which is to help protect various regions of American people from dangerous, or destructive flooding. Then this is a process to compile, and collect wastewater from every house, and commercial facility in the country which may be close to a river, lake, ocean, or any factor of groundwater.

To recognize small, medium, or large city sanitary districts which are a diversified geographical resource of public monopolized government operations, there is a factual concern that consisted of 4 major lawful issues that are important. Those factors within issues are the treatment, and or processing of (1) wastewater, (2) storm water, (3) the infrastructure, and (4) public health and safety disciplines. Observing that the largest cities have challenges of larger populations and facilities, the smaller cities and towns, dill with a lower capacity of people, and facilities that includes their values of "economic, and financial" resources. Most of these industrial wastewater facilities are regulated by their individual states, and most local government legislative values, therefore this determines if vital upgrades will be done in a timely fashion. The effort of some upgrades had stalled in some cities and towns worse than others (c/o economic decisions) which the American Society of Civil Engineers has observed this issue to be a strong lack of infrastructure progress that needs to improve.

Throughout the United States during the 1990s various concerns have consisted of an infrastructure of sewers which has been recognized as a tremendous problem in numerous American cities, towns, and various states. The city of Chicago and its Metropolitan Water Reclamation District of Greater Chicago which the original name was the Sanitary District of Chicago is one of the largest wastewater treatment plants in the country. The city of Chicago which has numerous obsolete sewers causing some of the largest sinkholes in America's mid-west is due to their enormous water and wastewater activity in the sub-grade utility system. In this northern part of Illinois they take in 1.5 billion gallons of wastewater a day. Then some other wastewater process operations in northwest Indiana observes Gary, Hammond, Highland, Griffith, Hobart and other cities, and towns to equate over 500 million gallons of wastewater a day as a combination of treatment facilities.

Observing government wastewater and reclamation between various major populated cities like New York City, Los Angeles, Dallas, Atlanta, and Miami the wastewater, and storm water collection to these largely populated cities are diversified, and tremendous. Understanding America, some parts of the northeast, and other potential flood prone regions should have been observed by the U.S. federal government to stabilize this problem. Then the concept of reclamation within reclaiming storm water use for certain treated water needs where considered for additional nature concerns. Understanding this, a city may provide water to non-human needs contrary to a level of treatment, and the disposal of extracted waste in a vital process for local municipalities. This is the understanding that rivers, lakes, and other waterways will increase their water levels with this process from government treated conditions of effluent water.

Los Angeles County has 11 municipal plants for wastewater, storm water, and reclamation purposes of consolidated treatment. Contrary to Los Angeles and the capacities of water in California, the city of Sacramento has consisted of the Shasta Dam for electricity, and reclamation. This hydroelectric dam controls water levels from the Sacramento River, and Valley. Therefore the indifference of the largest cities is that there are hundreds of smaller cities and towns that consist of the same engineering, construction, and government values of wastewater, and storm water reclamation replacing water back into lakes, rivers or irrigation. Understanding this process various business, social, and regulation matters become diversified for government agencies like the Bureau of Reclamation.

The factor of storm water in northern Illinois and northwest Indiana has been tremendous with some complacent solutions for certain parts of the Little Calumet River between northern Indiana, and Illinois. Also this includes the Des Plaines River, and the Fox River of northern Illinois. Observing the Des Plaines River this is a storm water issues that every few years a vast amount of citizens lose an enormous amount of assets due to these cresting rivers with flooding waters. These are a few infrastructure issues of storm water management that are far behind water retention standards, and this has been costing citizens an enormous amount of extra money to live in these areas. Even with the Little Calumet River requiring over $100 million of dollars of (Indiana) state and federal funded upgrades, it still requires work that northwest Indiana must be observant about. This concern is due to the regions flood damages in 2008, and now potential damage to the infrastructure of obsolete roads, and bridges that intersect with the river.

Understanding the American system of monopolized business as various companies have certain U.S. Department of Defense contracts a vast amount of product patents exist. Then they are quite serious about protecting these patents, so understanding this monopolizing is not easily considered. A good example is Raytheon Corporation with the Patriot missile system which has not been easily matched. Also U.S. Anti-Trust laws within the present day of 2013 have caused an equation for these business disciplines to have equality, professionalism, and fairness, but some U.S. Constitutional issues still apply.

Contrary to the U.S. Post Office, and certain telephone companies like Verizon the U.S. Department of Defense has a resource of decisions to hire contractors or review bids, and or proposals. Then this is where no anyone business is to easily be a defense monopoly that is rare to happen without common values of a patent. Decades ago corporate businesses like American Telephone and Telegraph Corporation, U.S. Steel Corporation, and Standard Oil Company where some of the few monopolies that were viable United States Department of Defense contractors of security. Other industry sectors of these businesses consisted of food, medicine, clothing, artillery, along with other manufactures of products. Understanding these businesses may not be at the capacity level of a monopoly, but they still find long term business success as well.

The U.S. Department of Defense has an equation (c/o a multi-billion dollar budget) that spends money on hundreds of contractors, and vendors. This list of businesses earn fairly good income (c/o tens to hundreds of billions of dollars a year), but these contractors take on some hard hits. Then they must work hard to keep their commitment, or they are usually restricted by law, and unprofessional or unqualified standards to conduct this resource of business. Even more sometimes they are subject to legal court matters, criticism, and or stiff competitive conflicts. Therefore even during a time of war (c/o 2002 to 2013) with one of the worse war-time economies in U.S. history certain monopolies will maintain business values. Observing any of these conflicts most corporate business will then go back to business as usual.

Doing business with the U.S. Department of Defense, and or the United States government is a valuable resource, and can consist of secured benefits. Numerous businesses such as General Electric Corporation, Raytheon Corporation, Northrop Grumman Corp, General Dynamics, and others are just a few with large contracts, and commitments to the U.S. Defense Department. Considering this diversified concept of defense contractors, these corporate businesses are usually equipped to appropriate the necessary products, and or services. Then with some of the most advanced resources of research and development in America, then therefore the products that they manufacture are sometimes component by-products of other products that keep America advanced in defense technology. Understanding this they may have some values of a monopoly on certain products, but they also maintain a good corporate and business relationship with other large companies, and the United States government.

CHAPTER SEVEN

Monopoly & Public Utility
Mergers & Acquisitions

An American Study Of Business & Monopolies

Monopoly & Public Utility Mergers & Acquisitions

The American society of business within monopolies, and public utilities has endured various mergers, acquisitions, and complex buyouts. It must be observed that some monopolies, and public utility mergers, and or buyouts have been tremendously complex that changed some product and service resources in the American society. These transactions have occurred in the American society with people having to adjust to economic difficulties that have led to some product and service changes, the control of patents, and employment concerns which occasionally had conflicts.

Considering the economic side of these acquisitions within mergers or buyouts their repercussion has been a vital factor to the economy in the United States. Then before and after the first decade of 2000 this has consisted of various good, bad, and or complex transactions. Therefore sometimes these transactions don't hold productive value, but they do work to occasionally provide better management, liquidity, or good services for the overall resource of American citizens if crime or greed is not a factor.

Considering public utility monopolies such as FirstEnergy Corp, Houston Natural Gas (c/o Enron), Commonwealth Edison (c/o Exelon Corp), and others like Northern Indiana Public Service Company (c/o Nisource) the concept of mergers has been tremendous. This is observed on a good and bad condition of value to make progress on the infrastructure in America with massive equipment earning additional income, and even most times their accounting standards. The accounting issue of these businesses became so conflicting with the "Enron and Arthur Andersen accounting scandal" that the U.S. government established the Sarbanes-Oxley Act to have better control over bookkeeping. Upon this observation these and other American utility companies are part of a multi-billion dollar industry which endured some good, and very bad times. Observing this, these mergers, and acquisitions were only a slight value of progress.

Most American public utility companies hold a level of stable economic assets, and the conditions of earnings from the regions they usually do business with consist of an enormous amount of customers. The massive amount of public utility company customers has made these secured and interesting investments helped offer additional resources to the good, bad, and even conflicting establishment of diversified investors. This then is part of the gain within controlling ownership of 1 or 2 of these monopolized businesses which gives another business owner managing capabilities to seek large investments, and borrow money with enormous assets to leverage. Then this becomes the reason the board of directors, and top level management officials have certain Securities & Exchange Commission (SEC) responsibilities which can include the input, and submittal of information to investors.

Enron Corporation was able to gain control of certain public utility companies, and leverage their assets to expand their business at tremendous rates. One of the problems at Enron Corporation consisted of them not being able to answer for $11 billion dollars of losses (c/o reporting $101 billion dollars in revenue in 2000) which caused them in 2001 to file for bankruptcy. During that time in 2001 Enron's corporate stock price fell from $85.00 a share to $0.30 a share which is unprecedented, and disastrous. This has been the consideration that Enron was started from a merger of "Houston Natural Gas, and InterNorth" which all together later became Enron Corporation with their "disastrous founder/CEO" Kenneth Lay.

Various companies like Houston Natural Gas, and then "Enron" with their merger agreement with Portland General Electric had conflicting similarities. These were public utility transactions that provided Enron Corp with an enormous market of customers that generated them fairly productive resources of greenmail, and cash liquidity with additional income earnings. Understanding this concentration of mergers became a tremendous loss for customers, some investors, a variation of employees, and the American system of courts with legislature which found vital public, and government reason to get involved, which means changes were inevitable. This becomes the extensive effort that the United States government had to make which consisted of severe cost within prosecution of the Enron corporate officials, and seizing all of their business assets. Also this government involvement consisted of an enormous amount of retired investors, retired employees, and employees who loss, their jobs, pensions, investments, and retirement savings as they depended on the financial, and overall future of the company.

Enron becoming an Energy Trading company is different from electric companies like Commonwealth Edison, Northern Indiana Public Service Company, Arizona Public Service Company, and somewhat FirstEnergy Corporation. These public utility companies were similar to Portland General Electric (before & after Enron) whom provided a region full of customers in Oregon with electric utility services without too many financial levels of disaster. What all of these public utility companies have in common is that they have involved themselves in corporate buyouts, and mergers upon which some have not truly helped the industry expand, and this included "not" improving the American economy. Considering this or any expansion has come slow, but effective to some values of discipline over the decades upon which had to be restored, and restructured. Then levels of efficiency may occur due to working with different levels of customers, and government.

Contrary to various good and bad public utility factual concerns, there overall systems of electrical power and natural gas distribution are most times upgraded, but some are still behind the times. This has conditionally been an issue with Pacific Gas & Electric Company upon where more financial companies did not help before a September 2010 fatal gas explosion. Considering this, other industry concerns near these core electric utility, and or gas companies have loss some control to financial companies.

These companies who have gained control of a percentage of regional public utilities income have reduced occupational and professional opportunities like within some engineering values. Then other issues consisted of some important standards like employee stock ownership plans that have become conflicting like government mandated health insurance. Observing these industry problems from the stability of these monopolized business operations is conflicting due to some professional engineering standards apart from financial standards. Then considering these changing times in America some professional disciplines still exist, but management must have logical commitments. Therefore this utility industry including the American system of government must be more careful in the future.

The establishment of FirstEnergy Corp with their present 2013 CEO Anthony Alexander is a combination of 10 electric utility companies compiled into one. They now have a managing presence in 7 states consisting of Ohio, Pennsylvania, West Virginia, Virginia, Maryland, New Jersey, and New York. There were 10 merged companies that created FirstEnergy within Ohio Edison Co, and its subsidiary Pennsylvania Power Co, whom merged into Centerior Energy Corp including their subsidiaries the Cleveland Electric Illuminating Co, and the Toledo Edison Company. Also during 2001 FirstEnergy merged with General Public Utilities Inc, and the Metropolitan Edison Company whom had part ownership in Three Mile Island nuclear plant. Others included their connection of ownership with New Jersey Central Power & Light Company, and the Pennsylvania Electric Company. Therefore between 1995 and 2002 this time frame consisted of a reduction of 7 to 10 publicly traded utility companies. Then as this applies to the American financial markets they have not been a major force to improve the overall economy.

The activity of FirstEnergy and a few others were companies that are managed by various businesses over the last 2 decades which consisted of some good and bad values. These are factors of an enormous amount of concerns especially as it applies to America's economy which has been in a recession for the last 7 years, and somewhat counting. The increase in parent company controlled business transactions is one of the major factors. Observing this, the first decade of 2000 between management, labor unions, and the government has consisted of the concentration of these companies having been the concern of economic balance, and logical control. With this understanding, most labor unions have good, and bad issues where the best decisions should not be to destroy the company, or even any individual small businesses.

Other acquisitions in American business have led to some merger and buyout issues that would control certain markets in America, and internationally. FirstEnergy Corporation, and Exelon Corporation seem to fit some of these merger/buyout active conditions, but they did not exist on a destructive path like WorldCom Corporation. The difference of these three corporations is that FirstEnergy Corp and Exelon Corp have gain control of various utility companies throughout the United States which consist of a mix of electricity, and natural gas distribution. This was also the factor of WorldCom Corporation (c/o telecommunication), and a few other corporate business concerns with different products, and services as they wanted to be the largest, and most controlling company in the world. Therefore this has led to conflicting problems, and then even levels of corporate destruction, and or a reduction of various businesses after some merger business activity failed.

Exelon Corporation was established in October of 2000 by a merger of PECO Energy Company, and Unicon whom operated in Philadelphia, and Chicago. Unicon had gained ownership in Commonwealth Edison of Chicago which came together with PECO Energy Co. as these activities created Exelon Corporation. Then the Exelon Corporation with their 2013 CEO Christopher Crain became even larger with an extensive market of electrical power distribution services with various facilities, and assets. Some of these assets consist of a majority ownership of 17 nuclear reactors, 10 nuclear power plants, and other energy generating resources such as wind, and solar energy. This activity removed Commonwealth Edison from being a publicly traded company similar to others like Northern Indiana Public Service Company with their new parent company Nisource.

Considering the acquisitions by FirstEnergy Corp, and Exelon Corp this is one consideration of why the U.S. Congress passed the Public Utility Holding Company Act (PUHCA) of 2005. These are public utility resources which became important to the fact that; the more advanced some technology become, the more regulation occasionally became important for this concentration of public utility resources. Also this being part of the Energy Policy Act of 2005, most PUHCA activity within laws gave the Federal Energy Regulatory Commission a limited role in allocating the cost of multi-state electric utility holding companies to individual operating subsidiaries. Therefore more public utility companies eliminated their business activity in one state, as they became more active in a different combination of other individual states.

Basically the Energy Policy Act of 2005 theoretically meant that lately electric utility companies would start doing business under larger parent companies like Nisource, Exelon, and FirstEnergy. These are similar issues to an insurance company like AIG with numerous subsidiaries, observing the concern that too many companies are becoming too big to fail, or even manage good. This became a financial resource, and conflict with less publicly held utility companies for smaller or other logical investors. Understanding the changing times in the American society this became similar to the repeal of the Glass Steagall Act within the banking industry, but public utilities consisted of more issues of industrial liabilities, and various patents. Then the factor of greed apart from productive professional standards, scientific principals and even employment opportunities suffered. This observation became a threat similar to the anger of people boycotting Wall Street firms during the year of 2008.

Contrary to anger against the financial markets one way American's in different states can recognize changes in the "Electrical Energy Generating and Distribution" industry is by the expansion of wind farms in most rural areas. Some things throughout this industry have not changed much with General Electric Corporation providing manufacturing, and the sales of wind turbines similar to years "ago and now" with electrical transformers. This division of General Electric Corp with their present CEO Jeffery Immelt, and their subsidiary of GE Energy has been also managed with value by John Krenicki the divisions President/CEO that has given the company a slight boost in sales. Therefore observing FirstEnergy, Exelon, Pacific Gas & Electric, and other regional monopolies they usually depend on, the stronger businesses have been consistent with these products from General Electric Corporation. Then this makes General Electric Corporation a strong constituent to most all American, and some foreign public utility monopolies.

Understanding large conglomerate businesses, and monopolies for electrical power distribution, and or various communication industry concerns, powerful connections, and corporate business relationships were established. General Electric Corporation being established from an Edison company during 1882 has kept a format of developing a vast array of consumer, and industry products. This makes their design, engineering, research, manufacturing, and sales an issue that is not easy to compete with for various other corporate businesses. Understanding this a limited amount of corporate businesses find themselves working together more than normal.

Contrary to General Electric, the changing or repealing of certain legislative factors of laws in the "Energy, Communication, and Banking" industries did not recently serve the American society very good. Even as Jeffery Immelt has had a good working relationship with President Barack Obama, and some others various important technology issues were recognized, or somewhat considered as deregulation has been an industry concern. This is valuable within the fact considering that General Electric Corporation has products that can be sold to every public utility electric company in America. Observing this other corporate businesses, and various public utility monopolies consist of different business liabilities, and responsibilities that are most all the time secured with these products.

Contrary to conglomerates like GE Corp, very few monopolies are bought out by bigger corporate businesses. This is totally indifferent from the conflicting American electric utility industry, and how they have been reorganized with various mergers. Standard Oil Company was a major example; besides Amoco Oil Corporation being bought out by BP and this was the result of Standard Oil Company being broken up by the American system of government.

As Standard Oil Company was one of the most "wealthy", in the world during the early 1900s, this brake up, and spin-off into various corporate activity was enforced by the United States government. Also this included some state government officials upon which this turn of events created other large oil companies. Besides some of their spin-off companies of Mobil, Exxon, Chevron, Imperial Oil, Socony, and Conoco this included other oil company brand names in America, and some worldwide. These have been some of the most complex transactions in American business, but some level of fairness, and equality were achieved. The only other comparison was the brake up, and spin-off disciplines of AT&T some 60 years later.

As products and services in America expanded in this well-developed society, enormous progress and prosperity within business was a value that could be achieved. This occurred within the good and bad of Standard Oil Company, American Telephone and Telegraph Corporation, and now the observed technological superiority of Microsoft Corporation. Actually these are similar business and technology expansion issues observed with valued competitors or constituents like IBM, and Apple computer. Bill Gates, Steve Jobs, and a few others in a vast amount of industries with various products have kept this level of capitalism alive in America. Michael Dell with Dell Incorporated is another business owner whom has created a multi-billion dollar computer company that manufactures an array of computers which most times have good sales, and income earnings.

Understanding a capitalist society becomes the valuable issue of people working hard on various products, research, management, and other business value concerns. Another part of this equation of capitalism is the social disciplines like "church, and state" with values of government. The church, certain organizations, and both the State and Federal Constitutional disciplines of government becomes important because they are moral, and relevant laws of the land, "by and for the people" of America. This vitally includes how they are part of the better resource of people that productively worked with these industry innovators of products, services, and our U.S. diversified business markets.

When America observes this real factor of "capitalism", businesses such as ExxonMobil, AT&T, Microsoft, Apple, and even General Electric are understood as astute corporate businesses that protect their overall operation. Then it is evaluated that they buy businesses, or conduct merger agreements with other companies that lead to stronger monopoly disciplines, or potential conglomerate levels of business. Contrary to these valuable factors of American cars, airplanes, shipping vessels, and thousands of other products which are factoring advancements; this is their own perceptional way of creating a well-developed society of business. Therefore the American society of corporate business, have made certain advancements, but some smaller businesses with various banks and some issues of employment have lately been an economic problem during the end of the 1st decade of 2000.

Diversified industries, and market disciplines that lead to various monopolies in America are a powerful consolidation of what people, and businesses spend money to pay for within what they consider vital. Monopolies, conglomerates, and even all types of public utilities are conditions of a capitalist society. This is a factor of small and large businesses that find opportunities to expand upon whom their owners make the best business decisions possible under any national or regional economic conditions. Between the laws that include U.S. Anti-Trust law issues and the Constitution a vast amount of the time these issues will help people including businesses prevail with prosperous growth, and logical expansion. Then considering these factors of complex crime, and or greed most times this becomes a resource of protection, and only occasionally factual condition that destroys their business.

Observing the good, and enormously bad of mergers, and acquisitions of the 1990s, and the 1st decade of 2000; the United States Securities and Exchange Commission (SEC) has been quite busy. Understanding the Securities Exchange Act of 1934 an enormous level of greed, manipulation, and fraud has been part of a destructive economic factor for millions of Americans upon which most of the people were managing, and saving money for a retirement, or their children's future education. Contrary to public utility economic disasters like Enron, and them owning Portland General Electric numerous financial crimes occurred. Then others like WorldCom; the housing market combined with some banking institutions made this the worse compounded economic events since the 1930s. Therefore it seems that every law that was established coming out of the 1930s had been overthrown, ignored, and or repealed without concern. This became the logic of what helped greedy people take America full speed backwards.

During a 2007 review of the recent American economic crisis, over $11 trillion dollars of household wealth vanished which means a good amount of people had problems paying their utility bills, and other commitments. It has been rare that monopolies and or public utility companies file for bankruptcy like with Enron Corporation, and WorldCom Corporation, but this was an added problem to make the economic crisis even more complex, and intense. This part of understanding included the cost of the United States going to war in the Middle East (c/o Iraq & Afghanistan) upon which the U.S. economy was being ripped apart from these, and other bad or deceptive business practices.

Businesses that expand are vital, but understanding the economy and war with at least 40 new skyscrapers in Chicago is a tremendous evaluation of hopeful economic business progress. This is similar to other large cities whom, have consisted of various checks and balances that did not add up appropriately. These were the factors in a watered down real estate market, and the trillions of dollars it will take for a logical economic recovery. This factor of an economic recovery will conditionally take up until 2025, "unless" an extreme expansion of business income earnings appears from "all American's", or for that fact from almost nowhere to be lawfully or easily considered.

Understanding a good American economy, bi-partisan government duties are vitally important, but also the corporate, and individual small and large issues of business in the United States must be pursued, and managed at a capitalized rate. These are legal and logical disciplines of their business duties, products, services, and sells within their chosen markets. This becomes important in most market businesses, and technology that are, or will be vital with various industries. These industries may consist of agriculture, computer science, healthcare, engineering for the infrastructure, automobiles, locomotive trains, and or aircrafts with an enormous amount of other products, and services.

Americans have found conditional values in companies like Seagate Technology, the conflicting Monsanto Company Inc, Kellogg Co, United Parcel Services Inc, Federal Express Corp, and a few others that establish discipline. Then this level of discipline applies to not just control of their chosen markets, but also a subject of law to be responsible, and liable to the American society. Therefore an equation of laws, and productive business activities including technology braking points have been proven as advancements become workable and common to everyday business, or in the American life we live.

Seagate Technology has become a common resource within their manufacturing of hard drives for computers since the late 1970s which has kept them in control of this market in America. Contrary to their present 2013 CEO Stephen Luczo, and their consolidation of founders Alan Shugart, Tom Mitchell, Doug Mahon, Finis Conner, and "Syed litikar" they became part of an expanding computer industry that needed important data storage components. It took Seagate Technology 29 years during 2008 to sale over a billion hard drives.

Observing 2008 to 2013 Seagate Technology doubled that number of hard drives sold, which consisted of another billion hard drives sold for a more diversified array of devices. Some of these devices were computers that included the sales of memory hard drives for streaming video, online shopping, and other heavy-lifting data services. These data storage devices consist of a high demand of information technology, and program operations that are produced through computer or device user resources. Therefore within the internet use of cell phones, laptops, computer tablet's, cameras, and other digital operating products the format of this memory storage component became another monopolizing necessity.

Business and technology expansions became tremendous at Seagate Technology which is part of a managing factor to control the company. This observation of memory, and data storage industry concerns consist of Seagate Technology gaining control of various similar corporate businesses. Then this provides an increase in their business level of production, and sales. Considering these market levels of determination Alan Shugart was very involved in his company Seagate Technology during 1989 when they completed the purchase of Control Data Corporation's "Imprimis" division. This became a valuable asset to the expansion of Seagate Technology observing that between the 1950s, and the 1970s Control Data Corporation made the fastest computers in the world, which were established from the UNIVAC's resource of technology format.

Other acquisitions that expanded Seagate Technology was their purchase of Maxtor Corporation in 2006, and the Samsung hard disk drive division in 2011. Between 1995 and 2005 the American society went through a computer, and computerized device industry bubble, and expansion which included the internet. With the help of Seagate Technology and other computer industry valued concerns more advanced memory hard drives were in technology device demand for computer data storage capacity needs. From there these corporate expansion values required the acquisitions within computer technology patents to compensate this industry resource of advanced concern. Understanding these acquisitions which gave them, and their present (2013) CEO Stephen Luczo additional market control, a larger array of products to manage, and sale became vital as they achieved a responsible level of capitalism.

Contrary to the corporate businesses like Seagate Technology, Microsoft Corp, Apple Inc, IBM, and or even TVA whom consisted of certain corporate businesses that were close to monopolization most have had some controversial issues. One of the more controversial major monopolizing businesses was Monsanto Company Incorporated (est 1901) which is a multinational biotechnology corporation with many business subsidiaries, and divisions. Their level of production besides genetically engineered seeds, and various herbicides has also been the first company with scientist to effectively research, and massively manufacture agriculture seeds, and even light emitting diodes (LEDs) which became an industry value. Also their most controversial manufactured chemical products were the insecticide DDT, PCB contaminates, Agent Orange, and other biological compounded chemicals. The compounds of Agent Orange became a big U.S. Defense Department controversial issue during, and after the Vietnam War between the late 1960s, and early 1970s.

Monsanto Co Inc was one of the top 10 U.S. chemical companies with its headquarters in Creve Coevr, Missouri contrary to their divesture (creating two corporate businesses) with mergers, acquisitions, and spin-off agreements. This consisted of an array of valued chemical business divisions, and companies like G.D. Searle & Company that was acquired by Monsanto in 1985 for $2.7 billion dollars. From this transaction NutraSweet Company was established as a subsidiary of Monsanto. During 1996 Monsanto acquired Agracetus, most of Calgen, and 40% of DEKALB Genetics Corporation. Then another anti-trust issue required Monsanto to conduct a spin-off that occurred in 1997 with their chemical, and fiber divisions becoming Solutia Inc.

As Monsanto sold off NutraSweet Company in 1999, they then merged with Pharmacia and Upjohn during an aggressive "Junk Bond and Merger" market. Then between the agriculture division, and the medical research division of Monsanto they developed the drug Celebrex. This FDA approved drug Celebrex was created for arthritis, and a few other illnesses which managed its way into the ownership control of Pharmacia a Sweden pharmaceutical business. In 2002 Pharmacia was bought out by Pfizer which became a completed deal in 2003.

From 2005 to 2008 Monsanto spent well above $2.8 billion dollars on Emergent (the 3rd largest U.S. cotton seed company), with its Stoneville and NexGen cotton brands. This transaction had U.S. Anti-Trust issues from the U.S. Department of Justice within requirements for approval. Then understanding this a transaction occurred with Monsanto Company Inc obligated to divest the Stoneville cotton business, and then it was sold to Bayer. The other requirement was to divest the NexGen cotton business as it was sold to Americot.

The divesture of the chemical businesses at Monsanto Company between 1997 and 2002 was a process of transition that made a consolidation of different business concerns. Another major level of divesture consisted of Monsanto removing, themselves from the "pig breeding" business which consisted of selling Monsanto Choice Genetics to Newsham Genetics LC. This divesture eliminated them from all swine-related patents, patent applications, and all related intellectual properties.

The business values at Monsanto consisted of doing business with the company Genentech Inc, and other biotech drug companies. Understanding these diversified chemical companies over the last few decades they have been part of complex arguments about all kinds of products from soft drinks to chemical weapons. This was part of the ration from the good, and bad of chemical products that were established from the cotton seed growing business to the pig breeding business which was factored as genetics. Therefore various scientific patents, patent applications, and the Food and Drug Administration (FDA) approvals with a variation of other researched products has become a common government procedure for these corporate businesses.

The American resource of market control, and or monopolized businesses, has been observed from Kellogg Company, United Parcel Service Inc (UPS), and a few others. This is due to the fact that both of these corporate businesses are strong and prosperous in America, and throughout a vast amount of places around the world. The Kellogg Company in this regard holds a monopoly discipline in a few foreign countries which is part of them manufacturing products in 18 countries (c/o 2013), and with marketable sales in 180 countries. A similar subject is observed within how UPS delivers over 15 million packages a day to slightly over 6 million customers in a worldwide capacity. As UPS has done business in more than 220 countries and territories, some of these international monopoly controlled markets have given them an economic and service level of appreciation with success. Therefore this becomes a value of responsible capitalism.

Both United Parcel Service Inc, and Kellogg Company over the recent decades have been active in various mergers, and buy out acquisitions. United Parcel Service Inc from 2001 to 2006 has bought out at least 9 domestic and foreign competitors, and or corporate businesses that has given them additional market and business access. Federal Express is their sole American competitor that has did somewhat the same in acquisitions, but they have not overcome the market discipline and competitive level of resources of UPS. The Kellogg Company in 2001 acquired Keebler Company, and other corporate businesses including Morningstar Farms. Also in 2012 they acquired Pringles potato crisps brands from Proctor & Gamble for $2.7 billion dollars in cash which made them the 2nd largest snack food company in the world behind PepsiCo Inc. Therefore as these monopolies and businesses have various commitments and goals their acquisitions, and business transactions will consistently be part of a productive business or be similar to a secured utility companies format of prosperity in America, and throughout the world.

CHAPTER EIGHT

Regulating American Monopolies & Industry

An American Study Of Business & Monopolies

Regulating American Monopolies & Industry

The American system of government regulating industry which, consist of a vast amount of monopolies, and various U.S. Anti-Trust laws has been part of a vital government, and business level of importance. This regulative transition before and after the first decade of 2000 has been like very few times in American history. Also this gives the American system of government a duty to apply regulation to balance the discipline, and equation of small and large businesses that appropriate safety, and fairness which includes the U.S. Constitutional use, and distribution of technology and various products which occasionally includes food.

Understanding that the American society of people has a lawful right to invest in various "nearly conditioned monopoly types of businesses" this makes the Securities and Exchange Commission (SEC) a logical part of regulatory discipline. Since Harvey Pitt and up to today with Mary Jo White the recent Chairperson of the SEC is composed of people with observed and conditional challenges. This is due to the fact that the SEC has not protected a certain amount of small investor's money good enough from various scandals which is a tremendous concern, and duty of vital responsibility.

Contrary to the Bernard Madoff scandal and some other "bad" investment bankers at this time Mary Jo White the Chairwoman of the SEC has become an interesting regulator upon which small or mid-sized investors will require lawful opportunities to find stability. Millions of Americans over the last 15 years have loss retirements, investments, and even their life savings at an old age. Then understanding young or old American people with ambition, it has become an economic uphill battle to establish a prosperous business in a vast amount of American regions. This is similar to the control of people like Warren Buffet (c/o BSNF), Carl Icahn (c/o Western Union), and tens of thousands of other small and large businesses and investors which sometimes includes their employees seeking financial advancements.

Understanding government regulatory issues of duty, most times they apply to products, and services with responsibilities by the people hoping to reduce the cause of dangerous problems, and economic conflicts. Contrary to these facts some of these business and government values have consisted of helpful conditions apart from Enron, WorldCom, and Ameritech that recently did not serve a good purpose to industry standards, and values. Then, these bad businesses provided help to "destroy" jobs, and various other business conditions which became part of a failing American economy.

Observing issues from bad or destructive business resources like Enron with Ken Lay, and or WorldCom with Bernie Ebbers, this becomes irrelevant in aiding the American consumers, investors, employees, and various business communities. Upon this observation more complex legislature came during the first decade of 2000 with the most regulated industries becoming banking, but the manufacturing, and telecommunication industry caused a level of suffering due to some conflicting values. These conflicts with diverse problems, and concerns also included an aging American infrastructure that became dangerous. With disaster after disaster the citizens and government paid the cost to recover from these massive corporate, and government conflicts of economic hard times. From the 9-11 terrorist attacks to hurricane Katrina, and hundreds of fatal manufacturing explosions and accidents, America was headed in a bad direction over a 15 year time span.

Today's concept of monopoly businesses like in the telecommunication, and computer software industries with various internet business levels of activity certain U.S. Constitutional law concerns and the need of various regulatory conditions apply. Ameritech Corporation contrary to Microsoft Corp, and International Business Machines (IBM) are just a few examples of how the highest courts had to review, and serve regulatory duties. This went along with various "information technology (IT)" businesses, and corporations that sometimes violate the 4th Amendment within obtaining information illegally. These issues of today are similar, but different from newly developed technology years ago which had amended circumstances. Considering today, communication and information is more advanced than that of the early 1900s, and during the expansion of the oil, and telephone industries as this has created some unlawful Constitutional standards of activity.

Upon logical expansion of technology today various factors have only been a slight conflict, and this understanding of the most important laws has provided an equation of regulation for various industries. These laws are updates to the interpretation of the U.S. Constitution, and other lawful product standards that can legally or conditionally apply to good, and bad advancements of technology use. An important example is how various people have found electronic devises to steal other people's money from ATM banking machines at the rate of $10s of millions of dollars in certain regions. Also this includes manipulative videos, or confidential information shown on the internet that causes defamation of a person's logical character, and sometimes provokes violence to various people. Therefore this is most times how corrections are needed. Then the resource of law becomes important in a lawfully developed society which should, and can maintain their progressive values of a fair, un-abusive, and prosperous society.

The valid interpretations of the U.S. Constitution, outlines a governed authority to Grant Power, Limit Power, and Protects Against the Abuse of Power. Understanding this, a vast amount of corporate businesses make a logical and strong effort to manufacture products that comply with government specifications. The abuse or conflict within government powers comes when the American people do not have good lawfully appropriated government standards. Considering this the resource of American people are victimized with a non-workable society of government that has to be replaced or repealed. Also this is due to an enormous amount of new products, and services that make up new diversified markets like computer software products, internet service satellites with cell phones, and cable television services. Considering these facts most all the time this requires some level of regulatory discipline from the executive, legislative, and judicial branches of "separated power" within the American system of government.

Understanding product specifications and regulation has created responsible railroad, airline, computer, and satellite industries some of the most advanced products, and services this is valuable. This also has occurred around the world and throughout the American society with some appropriate progress. Even though railroads are not perfect the Hobbs Act was passed by the U.S. Congress to enforce laws against robbery and extortion with some labor unions in mind. This was progress that has been part of the secured shipping of diversified products which made good sense. These are factors which government continues to need to logically enforce, and establish with various legislature. Then with these industries, and new technology this requires laws which can be effective for a stable society of equality, or a, repeal to the law that may become important. Also these laws control good and bad activity which becomes appropriate support for the American general public, but more still needs to be done due to most arbitrary conditions of the internet, and satellite technology.

Two main parts of the United States federal government that are active with railroad companies consist of the Federal Railroad Administration, and the Surface Transportation Board, upon which both are part of the United States Department of Transportation. The managing of the Federal Railroad Administration at this time with Joseph Szabo's administrative duties are part of a hopeful commitment to keep logical regulation in a complete order of business with technology trends. Also during 2013 the Surface Transportation Board consisted of Daniel Elliott III, Charles Nottingham, and Francis Mulvey which is still in the process of establishing government concerns since this board was newly established in 1996. These issues and duties under Steven Chu of the U.S. Department of Energy with President Barack Obama has consisted of similar concerns except for conflicting investment banking matters.

Understanding the U.S. Department of Transportation which is slightly different from the Federal Communication Commission, and the U.S. Department of Energy most board and administration duties with government issues take up an enormous amount of resources. Between the Presidents of George Bush, and Barack Obama and their administrations the concept of government effectiveness has been recognized most times after certain tragedies. These tragedies have occurred with distribution, but some military efforts like the killing of Osama bin Laden had been long term awaited welcoming news for most Americans. Considering this, numerous accidents and terrorist plots have finally been taken under control, and considered vital as this is good for our American society, the transportation industry, and others.

As the railroad industry has been one of the oldest upon critical industries of a regulatory capacity in America, their magnitude of classified railroads has endured a good and bad diversion approaching the year 2010. These Class I, II, & III specifications with advancements of railroads has been part of their financial competitive nature. This resource of business has appropriated productive services that have most times been important to government, and industry. Contrary to conflict, these fairly productive issues of U.S. regulatory disciplines have consisted of the financial markets in America, and some internationally whom have put conflicting money "invested" into various Class III railroad businesses. This therefore is a concern to control railroad activity in America. Then besides safety standards some investors only partly or lawfully wanted to help the disciplines of good management change for various good or bad reasons.

The format of conflicting railroad concerns existed for logical business expansion, but a somewhat loss occurred with the buyout effort of numerous Class III railroads by RailAmerica Inc who existed from 1986 to 2010. One of their vitally important acquisition approvals was delayed by the Surface Transportation Board, therefore a lack of sustainable managing seem to take RailAmerica Inc slowly out of business. This has been quite different from a smaller Class I railroad company like the Kansas City Southern Railway Company (KCS) that has operated in a productive capacity. The KCS Railway Company has done this by being an active transportation company from the southern or lower mid-west of America to Mexico. Then these factual levels of business become a logic of consolidated control for appropriate regulation, and astute management with expanding potential.

Various parts of the short route distribution of products with the less expensive Class III distance of transporting, and distributing products consisted of activities within an enormous amount of local railroads. These local distribution matters of travel ether as an independently owned company, or as a corporate owned operation such as the extent of Alcoa Co maintaining railroad land was the connection and distribution of corporate materials, and products. Between Pennsylvania, Michigan, Indiana, Ohio, and Illinois the railroad business became extensive for passenger, and more so fright distribution. Therefore controlling various large or active business operations with products like steel, aluminum, automobiles, coal and even cattle this process is a helpful part of these industry resources.

Observing railroad companies they occasionally have been observed as a potential concern of monopolizing to control markets like shipping coal, chemicals, other small and large items, and the ownership of land. Also their business activity from state to state by doing business within diversified industries, and various regions consist of laws, and a resource of responsibility within long distance travel. These are values of business that are part of a consolidation of different business concerns that are the workmanship of corporate products from sometimes small resourceful businesses, and that are important to government tax revenue with other business regulated values.

The resource of specifications and regulation has been endured with some ups and downs in Class I, II, & III railroads for over a century. These are business transportation short and long distance travel resource conditions with economic levels of business activity in the American railroad sector of industry. This has been part of government's diversified equation of railroad classifications which started in 1911 by reports from the Interstate Commerce Commission. Today's railroad companies like Burlington Northern & Santa Fe (BNSF), Union Pacific, and Norfolk Southern are just a few large Class I fright railroad businesses that have had to endure laws, and regulatory standards. Their enormous amount of distance of tracks averages 20,000 to 35,000 miles with multiple cars of fright pulled by specified locomotives. An appropriate example is how Ford Motor Company occasionally may ship a massive amount of vehicles from Mexico to or from Chicago, Illinois or to Canada contrary to some 50 other far away states.

The railroad industry has observed their economic and financial levels of managing a large business operation with good, bad, and competitive times. On a vast amount of occasions this is due to important regulation which may have existed with industry wide problems or the fault of a conductor that needs correcting. This was also recognized with the Exxon Valdez oil tanker's captain that caused a massive oil spill in the Gulf of Alaska. Contrary to the oil industry Union Pacific railroad had an accident in Texas during 2004 which killed 3 people, and put 43 other people in the hospital from the spill of chlorine. This train accident cost $7 million dollars to clean up with Texas Governor Rick Perry and Senator Kay Hutchison pushing for different, and improved regulated procedures.

Understanding massive small and large train accidents, American transportation, and more so railroad standards and regulation were observed as outdated or slightly inaccurate upon updates. These issues go back further than most other conditions of legislature such as with the Railroad Act of 1862. Therefore these are relevant concerns that even consist of a level of transportation industry accidents which have taken people's lives, contaminated land and water with chemicals, and which have cost enormous amounts of money to correct.

Contrary to good and bad regulation the local, state, and or federal government gets involved as railroad companies like Union Pacific, and BNSF find levels of importance in upgrading their corporate businesses. These become industry standards that occasionally have faults. Also these become factual business responsibilities as Union Pacific with their company president James Young making an effort in expanding their business, and to apply with government regulators. Understanding this in railroad businesses, and some other business concerns working with government, most of these issues apply to safety if all precautions are considered. This includes their extensive level of heavy railroad equipment for fright or passenger trains, and for people living near railroads, or motorist and pedestrians obeying the railroad crossing at intersections.

Observing the railroad business within them traveling to a vast amount of places throughout the United States, this consist of resourceful regulation and standards. This is factual in them delivering almost any kind of product fright, or their capability to carry people safely with regulatory standards of importance. These issues have consisted of a variety of specifically designed railroad cars, and some advanced railroad cars for specified use. Just like car, truck, boat, airplane, and bus parts various railroad train parts and train cars consist of important specifications that are documented with the U.S. Department of Transportation. Then a specification with trains exist within the location of chemical, and other train cars that are different for coal, cattle, or shipping product procedures. This even includes how they eliminated the necessity of the caboose railcar that consisted of the crew at the rear of a freight train. Therefore numerous changes have occurred with this issue of divesture within advanced technology.

As America engages in passenger transportation one company besides mass transit subway systems has been the large conflicting, but U.S. government funded Amtrak system of passenger trains. The intercity business activity of Amtrak has been maintained with certain levels of government control since 1971. Amtrak originated from passenger train activity in the 1920s as a very popular resource of travel which became an advantage to Americans going from state to state, or within complex intercity travel. This also included how things changed after the 1930s with the U.S. government establishing the National Highway System for massive vehicle use which required better roads, and other programs. Also these government programs developed airports for transportation by aircrafts. Even from 1916 when the United States had 254,251 miles of railroad track, "which has been reduced" to 140,695 miles by the year 2007 more diversified transportation has occurred.

Amtrak like some other large railroad companies or corporations has the potential to be a monopoly which the U.S. government understands in a very discrete and responsible way. This is the consideration of how they control a certain amount of Amtrak subsidiary train routes, and business matters. The parent company of Amtrak being the National Railroad Passenger Corporation oversees an enormous amount of routes with 2,142 railway cars, and 425 locomotives as of 2013. Therefore this gives their 20,000 employees, and their president Joseph Boardman a working capacity of government owned, and controlled transportation market disciplines.

The establishment of the telegraph with utility poles also goes back a long way with government support and regulation which made public policy a duty as this industry continued to advance. Understanding the telegraph, the telephone, and now satellites with cell phones; certain utility poles are now adjusted with cell phone towers. Observing the first 2 decades of 2000 this became an industry that has transitioned a level of expanded wireless communication and various internet services in a worldwide capacity. This is slightly different concerning Western Union Company upon which Carl Icahn has been a major investor during their initial public offering. The format of the telegraph, which was patented by Ezra Cornell, and more so Samuel Moses has led to Cornell's 160 plus years of established business operating outcomes of Western Union Company. Just a few additional major government regulators of concern have been the FCC, the SEC, certain contract work with the U.S Department of Defense, and some arguments throughout the courts with some helpful disciplines of the U.S. Department of Justice.

Observing the telegraph, and the telephone these have been patents like others with legal regulation, and arguments since the 1930s, and the 1940s. These issues where part of establishing the Federal Communication Commission (FCC) which is a regulator that now in 2013 has recognized diversified patents, and other communication issues. Between Western Union Company, GTE, AT&T, Microsoft, Netscape, and a few other corporate businesses they have consisted of numerous court proceedings with arguments. These issues of communication regulation, by the United States government includes the expansion of cell phones, and the internet business activities of the American society in a good, and bad capacity. These arguments already include the concept of considered good and bad law violations from patent laws, to obtaining information illegally within trying to control people and markets with technology.

The Federal Communication Commission in the 2nd decade of 2000 has keyed in on 7 vital bureaus. These bureaus are Consumer & Government Affairs, Enforcement, International, Media, Wireless Telecommunications, Wireline Competition, and the newly Public Safety and Homeland Security commission. Enron Corporation tried to capitalize on Broadband, but as an energy trading company they had too many uncoordinated technology, and business issues which turned up to be fraud infested. Enron Corporation was prominent when broadband, the internet and other communication industry matters became popular social and business issues. Therefore with them having a strong holding in the utility monopolized sector of businesses this gave them more economic leverage to market and control some of these services like a lawfully productive business to invest in.

Contrary to the FCC also regulating broadband they have conducted "some" of their business properly with what I most critically understand as important being possibly Consumer & Government Affairs. This becomes the issue as government and corporate officials thrive to vitally be involved in obtaining information illegally, "similar to some in the media with ambition for press news stories that have existed for the last 100 years. Also in government similar to the Watergate scandal which lately has destroyed some small American businesses illegal and hazardous commercial satellite activities have been out of control. Then as they destroyed citizens, and some small responsible businesses, this was a concept of unconstitutional conflicts that took Americans backwards. Critically they even ignored an enemy foreign agenda to kill Americans on September 11, 2001 with an extension of other problems.

As the Federal Communication Commission, and the Securities & Exchange Commission (SEC) did not care or enforce the laws against Ameritech Corporation with William Daly, and a few others causing problems to individuals in the mid-west states, part of America got worse. Then as a result various long time American citizens as small investors, and small business owners suffered tremendously. These Americans were sometimes threatened to the likes of being called criminals, victimized by crime, and therefore their hard work was taken in vain which severely hurt the black community of businesses, and certain other people.

Observing Ameritech Corporation, their monopolized business caused various problems along with a few others which took in less or conflicting income, and then paid or caused "less" tax revenue to be locally generated. After 8 to 10 years they failed with their only hope of survival becoming the support of AT&T (c/o SBC) as a parent company bailout, and the divesture of Ameritech. This became one of the concerns of government, and more so certain factors of monopolized business issues that had a losing effect on the overall American society. Considering this, numerous businesses started to fail with an extensive level of violent crime making gangs (fraternized) a conflicting, and destructive outcome in the mid-western states and a vast amount of other parts of America. Therefore to monopolize is also a factor to control a good or occasionally bad format of business for the American society, and citizens.

The regulatory condition of the Federal Communication Commission and the comparison of the U.S. Department of Commerce is where the Interstate Commerce Commission was eliminated. This has created issues that have slightly or conditionally taken some Americans backwards. As this applies to U.S. domestic and international monopolies the loss of U.S. Commerce Security Ron Brown was a tipping point between greed, and deceitful black and white American businesspeople. Considering he died in an airplane crash this was a time in American history where government, and "some" corporate businesses became complacent. Also during this time in the 1990s up to 2000 more low level jobs within businesses like Service Merchandise, Montgomery Ward's, Zayre Department stores, and other businesses where pushed into economic losses, and closed. Therefore they were affected negatively which left hundreds of thousands of employees out of work with slim changes of a logical retirement.

Understanding the resource of regulating monopolies observing the 1900s, and 2000 is part of how the American society of government must keep various people from unlawfully controlling other innocent citizens. This also includes how people gain prosperity within accumulating various assets to work or own a small expanding business or live a comfortable life. The 14th Amendment of the United States Constitution outlines and state's ; that "No state (c/o people) should deprive any person of life, liberty, or property without due process of law; nor deny to any person within its Jurisdiction the equal protection of the laws. Therefore the people along with small, large or corporate businesses and especially government have a sworn duty to comply, and enforce this lawful resource of equality, and way of life in the American society.

CHAPTER NINE

The Control Of U.S. & International Markets

An American Study Of Business & Monopolies

The Control Of U.S. & International Markets

The business and monopoly control of markets in the United States, and internationally have been a changing factor of products, services, and government resources. This usually comes from companies like U.S. Steel, Kellogg, General Electric, Boeing, Exxon, General Motors, Ford, Microsoft, Apple, Sperry, IBM, UPS, and a few others. In the same resource of concern some of these corporate businesses have changed to the extent of merger transactions, or buying out other corporate businesses to maintain stable liquidity, which sometimes is due to unstable foreign markets. Contrary to unstable foreign markets, and issues of liquidity these companies still make advancements in technology, and hold a strong presence in various markets in America.

Since the late 1800s, and more so today during 2013 American, and international business has changed with various good, and bad developing nations. Understanding this, other countries have been a careful and conflicting process of conditional trade agreements which even includes American corporation's selling certain products to foreign governments. Microsoft Corp, and Apple Inc have developed and manufactured some of the more complex, and popular corporate products which is based on various media informative matters. Conditionally these two companies and a few others have actually cornered markets in most developed regions of the world with their products. Even more so this is where Microsoft Corp has an edge with computer programs within most all computer operating systems.

A vast amount of international trade, relations, and business issues have been regulated by the Federal Trade Commission with some observation from the U.S. Congress, and the United Nations. Then even various presidents and the U.S. Congress occasionally make logical efforts to get involved. Their level of involvement is even similar to American hostages in the late 1980s in Tehran. This included the Iran-Contra scandal and affair along with other issues recently where American employed contractors or workers were stationed internationally in or near active war zones. These sometimes deadly events can be transmitted thru communication networks, but some international conflicts are dangerous, and do require assistance from the U.S. Department of Defense, and United Nation (U.N.) Peacekeepers.

The activity of the U.N. is commissioned to lawfully protecting some normal business, and more so civilians in America, and then distinctively in undeveloped countries internationally. This was observed with the sad Iraqi leadership within Saddam Hussein's invasion of Kuwait with a worldwide oil industry. Also, the U.N. prosecution of Slobodan Milosevic (Europe), and Foday Sankoh (West-Africa) by U.N. officials for war crimes and terrorizing international civilians. This also includes low level developing countries where other issues of tragedy have occurred.

During tremendous conflicts observing the late 1980s with President George H W Bush's tenure became very active in international conflicts. Considering these factors up to the George W Bush, and Barack Obama administrations of today, the format of decisions against terrorism has consisted of certain measures to eliminate U.S. levels of weakness. Then some other issues where ignored, and only became important when factors of a disaster occurred. Understanding this, a vast amount of international conflicts have been interrupted, and disrupted the "domestic tranquility of the American society".

During the 1970s, and 1980s Japanese trade to the United States consisted of car companies like Toyota, and Nissan; which then included electronic companies with products from Samsung and other businesses. These foreign products became popular and financially prosperous in America with an enormous amount of revenue going back to Japan. Upon this observation some "European cars" considering BMW and Mercedes in America had been around for decades longer then the 1980s. Then this overall business concern became part of the aggressive and careful discipline of international markets with trade conditions of logical agreements.

As foreign products prospered an enormous amount corporate business and "public opinions from Americans" became relatively important. These were opinions about the amount of products being imported from various foreign countries which conflicted with the American economy. Then understanding these opinions that are important 1st Amendment Rights as citizens provided a logic to appropriate their concerns to the U.S. system of government as it applies to industry, a resource of major issues was recognized. Due to the American people's observation, this becomes their evaluation about employment, and business opportunities in a country that is considered to be "for the People, and by the People".

Observing the "Made In America" label this has played a big role in the economy, and throughout many levels of a money circulation throughout most diversified communities in the United States. As it applies to monopolies during the first decade of 2000 major cities have fallen on hard times due to factory closings, and extensive bankruptcies. A few examples of these cities are Chicago, IL, Detroit, MI, Harrisburg, PA, and various other steel industry related concerns similar to Gary, Indiana. Nevertheless a select group of corporate businesses continue to advance in America, and occasionally in other foreign countries. Then this becomes the factor of monopolies like public utilities, and market controlling businesses with value that holds a certain percentage of the U.S. economy stable.

Understanding a concept of bankruptcy in small, large or corporate businesses has only slightly affected monopolies such as electric, water, gas, wastewater, and some communication public utilities to an economic change which has affected America. During 2007 this was also observed in a banking industry with a credit default crisis, and a foreclosure crisis effecting millions of Americans. This became a problem to anyone who could not pay high taxes that had to be debated or who were subjected to increasingly hard economic times. Also this included "underwater mortgages" which were not occasionally an issue of logical compensation to a bank. Then this consolidation to certain American banking establishments put more Americans out of business around the year 2007. Therefore they had more bad loans, then good loans that negatively affected more banking establishment's income earnings.

Observing commercial real estate which suffered tremendously in the last half of 2000 to 2010 in places like Chicago, severe economic losses occurred. This problem was observed with major effects in other cities and states where tremendous economic suffering was slightly different. These effects were also troublesome in California, Nevada, and Arizona as this market consisted of damages to assets that has been real conflicting and "bad". This market of real estate and banking also consisted of some foreign investments in a crisis. Some crisis within conflict consisted of people that did not take careful concern of some responsible investments in their own communities. This also applies to restructuring these overall market problems, which helps the American system of government with operating funds from tax revenue which lately has been severely affected.

The American system of government had to restructure to the extent of sequestration or conflicting government budget cuts. This caused many levels of changes for people, and adjustments within spending habits or activities in government resources. Affordable housing from the federal government even became a major program that was cut severely from their budget. Therefore various people in America whom had a need within having to restructure their lives, and how to understand when to hold "government, and other businesses accountable", became a judgment of their own determined capacity.

The United States government with a struggling economy from numerous small, and large corporate businesses, and monopolized business resources have somewhat determined that the American people need various opportunities of advancement. As this was observed, the good and bad of immigration has become a serious factor which from Mexico to Iraq has consisted of concerns ranging from "illegal drugs" to "terrorism". Considering this we find the American system of government making an effort to control good, bad, or illegal domestic trade, and international trade conditions. These have been trade factors that even consist of "international investments" that have led to "international terror". Therefore regulation of all market's become important to protect the American society of appropriate values.

An American resource of discipline is important with small business expansion which has been logical for large corporate activity like at Kellogg Company as they offer numerous brands of cereal in most small and large grocery stores. Observing them on an international scale their recent CEO John Bryant, and their former CEO Jim Jenness have maintained experience in these foreign markets. That experience is valid as they manufacture products in 18 countries with marketable sales in more than 180 countries. This is part of an extensive workforce of employees, and a diversified level of managing business in various countries where laws are slightly different, and they seldom speak English. Therefore their control with market values are close to monopoly resource conditions, but Kellogg's market position consist of good or top level name brand breakfast products, and snack food items. This then keeps people throughout the world buying their popular and most times nutritious products.

Another comparison of market controlling businesses, and government owned operations has been the competitive business relations between the U.S. Post Office, Federal Express Corporation, and United Parcel Service Inc (UPS) which is quite broad. Between the years of 2007 to 2010 all three of these business delivery operating entities suffered during the late 2000 recent economic recession. UPS as stated by their CEO Scott Davis with his team of employees whom operate in over 200 countries managed to recreate economic earnings to over $49 billion dollars. The U.S. Post Office with their capability to send letters, and packages anywhere during 2011 with their Post Master General; Patrick Donaho has been subjected to the decision to close numerous facilities, and eliminate Saturday mail delivery. Federal Express Corporation has been pulling up a strong rear position between the three with merger and buyout activity which has given them additional parts of the market in America, and throughout the world.

Observing an American level of industry activity in corporate delivery businesses has been a factual condition of good, and bad foreign related matters of social discipline. Foreign government issues has played an important role in how various business issues, and delivery concerns have existed in such places as in North Africa, and the Middle East. Muammar Gaddafi the former president of Libya before his violent death caused an outrageous level of harm to his citizen's which was threatening to employees of businesses, and contractors from America. These were the additional complex problems of working in that region of North Africa. Therefore as Corporate American delivery companies including sometimes the U.S. Postal Service, who delivers mail, and packages throughout these complex regions, "emailing" has become somewhat a safe solution, but "letters and packages" are still a vital priority.

Many companies in America ship their products themselves to retail stores or use a delivery contractor. Two other sectors of industry in America that hold large markets domestically, and internationally are the oil, and pharmaceutical sectors of business. Pharmaceutical companies usually hold patents on various products that give them occasionally monopolized control on certain medications which lately has somewhat been a worldwide value. Considering this the largest pharmaceutical companies like Merck & Company, Pfizer Inc, and Eli Lilly & Company that markets, sales, and sometimes donates various medicines in international emergencies becomes valuable to saving people's lives. These companies hold strong levels of market share due to the professional health care demand for various medicines that doctors of internal medicine recommend, and need for their patents.

Professionals of different trades all over the world in developed countries have concerns, and needs for various products. Contrary to foreign made products some American products are occasionally in big demand. Over the years some communist countries like China at one time rarely allowed products from other countries to enter their markets, or on various occasions these products was not easily excepted. Therefore international trade has become a complex value, but the cost to manufacture these products, and maintain sales which includes earnings has been part of a transitional cost of living equation.

China, Japan, and sometimes India are part of a currency equation of not excepting, or buying various products. This is a complex factor as they have large populations and circumstantial products that are required for certain procedures, but American products are still conditionally expensive, and then they are rarely in big demand in poor or economically distressed countries. Without a large demand for products, some corporate businesses from Kentucky Fried Chicken to Ford Motor Company make decisions on what will be cost effective in foreign market establishment of business. If they are affordable products then the supply and demand is valid to consumers at a level of business that is responsible to the overall production of items, and any overhead cost.

Two corporate businesses with affordable products worldwide have been the Coca Cola Company, and PepsiCo Inc., which both also own other product brands that are popular in America, and also known internationally. Considering this there is no part of the United States, and most parts of the world that Coca Cola, and or PepsiCo can't be found in stores, and most times that includes a soda product for a reasonable, or logical price. These are multi-billion dollar companies that protect their product brands legally, but also they compete internationally to keep their market share. Then as they do business in hundreds of other countries with their earnings that are extensive, they maintain a logical format of business which includes the equation, and issue of the popularity, and a cost factor of this product that is acceptable most everywhere.

The Coca Cola Company with their present CEO Muhtar Kent during 2012 had a corporate net income of $9.1 billion dollars. Understanding this, their operating income during the same period consisted of more than 500 brand names with their total amount of assets being valued at $86.17 billion dollars which is part of having market control. In comparison PepsiCo Inc with their recent CEO Indra Nooyi during 2011 had a corporate net income of $6.2 billion dollars, which helped them move further, and also establish $72.88 billion dollars in total assets. Therefore these corporate businesses maintain strong presence in American industry, and worldwide which is also part of how they have invested, and "bought out" certain food chains, soft drink beverage brands, and pleased customers in numerous nations.

An enormous effort is observed within the production and sales of American cars, and various other products, but Boeing Corp airplane manufactures have somewhat been part of international industry standards. Boeing Corporation's most aggressive international competitor is Airbus which is a French company that holds a large part of this market with Boeing. As both of these corporate manufacturing businesses each hold close to 40 plus percent of this international market, there is an enormous amount of liability, and money involved. Then, it is understood that these large ticket items become relevant airline corporate business assets.

As large and profitable airline companies operate in a worldwide airline industry the use of these aircrafts are relevant to an overall level of U.S. domestic and international travel. Along with international travel it has also brought international terrorism to a frontier that the U.S. government has seen before, but that they failed to prevent on September 11, 2001 which includes other conflicts. Considering these facts the U.S. government had to spend more money on creating the Transportation Security Administration (TSA) with the Department of Homeland Security to reduce or eliminate terrorist acts in air travel. Therefore the format of international markets becomes a competitive, and complex issue (c/o not just Boeing & Airbus), but also for various airline travel companies. Then these resources of transportation disciplines most times are a factor of numerous well developed countries with levels of properly managed currency. This then can also maintain responsible levels of air travel, and secured safety.

Contrary to Boeing selling aircrafts worldwide, a few international business transactions consisted of bad circumstances. One major issue consisted of a large American investment blunder involved with Enron Corporation with joint agreements between General Electric Corporation, and Bechtel Corporation that occurred from the U.S. to a project in India. The Dabhol Power Company (c/o India) was formed by Enron Corp for $20 billion dollars which became one of Enron's most complex schemes, and failures. This was the factor of Enron Corporation leading the process of building a technologically advanced energy plant with General Electric equipment which was a plant designed by engineers from Bechtel Corporation. Observing Bechtel Corporation and even General Electric Corp with their last two CEO's Jack Welch and Jeffery Immelt has consisted of one of GE's worse business decisions since the 1970s.

The Dabhol Power plant (c/o Enron) is where GE even having a worldwide resource of business disciplines and sales consisted of GE taking a tremendous financial hit. This was due to Enron Corp not being legitimate with certain American business transactions. Then their international business with officials like CEO Kenneth Lay, and Sharon Watkins of "Enron Global Finance" made billions of dollars of transactions which added to some the worse investments in American history. Contrary to various Enron's scandals in California and other American states these international and domestic problems of finance became a big part of the recent financial problems to the American economy. Therefore this then included their effort of insecurity to do business in America, and other countries.

The concept of large ticket corporate American business items to foreign businesses or government within various countries is more of a challenge then less expensive or smaller complex items. Considering this observation of the economy and the format of being a developed foreign country is the determination of whether an American business can survive economically from doing business with that country. Understanding this, even the most prosperous monopolies rarely exist in undeveloped or unstable countries. Therefore if there is no market to "maintain or control", then they have a logical concern not to easily do business in that country.

As it is observed with American corporate business or select small business operations the consideration of a monopoly or control of a foreign market is truly complex. This is observed due to the fact that international laws and languages are slightly different with the opinions, and attitude of the majority of those foreign people. The diversion of people and their purchasing power within the economic stability of that foreign nation is a vital factor to determine if any American or foreign business competitor can gain a level of control in those markets. Therefore popularity, and adjustable business value's to the currency with various opportunities becomes an important factor and equation for progress.

CHAPTER TEN

The American Economy & Monopolies

An American Study Of Business & Monopolies

The American Economy & Monopolies

The economy in America has been generally supported by numerous industries consisting of small, and or large corporate operating businesses which includes a variation of monopolies. How monopolies in America provide products, commodities, and more so services has been part of a constant stream of "business, and government revenue". This is similar to the sales and services of gas, electric, telecommunication, water, and wastewater products with customer service agreements. Observing this factor, it is conditionally based on residential and commercial customers that all ways pay their bills contrary to those people who don't pay, or that are unable to maintain this conditional format of obligations. Therefore the, economic, and utility format of companies are faced with a financial problem contrary to businesses that expand.

The concept of public utilities are normally complex with large investments lately during the 1st decade of 2000 as they alone are not enough to help the U.S. economy stabilize. Another part of stabilizing the U.S. economy is tax revenue that funds local municipal governments. These are tax revenue funds that must be managed properly which is vital for the citizens to have appropriate government services, and logical support. Understanding this, other industries contrary to local or regional monopolies have a concern to be more productively involved with investments which is a part of prosperous business, and U.S. economic disciplines for expansion. Considering these factors of the U.S. economy some businesses are achieving record levels of earnings which is valuable to an economic cycle.

As the American economy in 2012 and 2013 still seems to be in recession certain investment banker "product/services" like derivatives and hedge funds, have been part of unequal investment opportunities. These are conditions in the financial markets that have been negatively affecting American small investors, some retired investors, or certain pension fund holding senior citizens, and some business owners. This becomes the consideration of small, and large business investors that work hard within the consideration that they "occasionally may" take a loss, but the largest equity fund investors take the lowest loss, if any! Considering this factor of private equity funds, and or hedge funds the economy in the United States during 2013 has not truly made it out of the 2007 recession. This will require some higher levels of prosperous business, but also small expanding businesses with a high level of overall effective operations with secured employment.

Besides the many public utility monopolies throughout American industry, most resourceful levels of logical business and government revenue have consisted of a diversified condition of good and more so bad business values. These bad economic standards of resource have consisted of the loss or mismanagement of corporate businesses such as Montgomery Ward's Corp, Service Merchandise, Zenith Corporation, Bethlehem Steel Corp, and Inland Steel Company. Even worse this includes the failure, and or restructuring of thousands of smaller businesses which most times depend on America's diversified banking institutions. Therefore the condition of stable markets with expanding businesses has been tremendously important, but they have been very slow and conflicting as it applies to the survival, startups, or expansion of business.

When monopolies in America are considered "important or vital" it usually consist of a characterized lack of "economic, and product competition". Then when monopolies are established or do occur, they are understood to have an ambition to produce items or services that lack viable substitute products. These products lately which includes more so certain services like the internet with computer operating systems, and wireless communication have been an arbitrary resource of conditional business. Then contrary to vital semi-monopolized utility services these become necessities like with products from Microsoft Corp, Apple Inc, and the services of Comcast, Verizon Communication, and AT&T. Upon this observation Bill Gates of Microsoft Corp, and Steve Jobs with Apple were part of intriguing individuals that expanded the user friendly concept of computers in America. Now with Microsoft's CEO Steve Ballmer with more than 8 major products, and Apple's CEO Tim Cook whom manages more than 10 diversified products this has brought economic expansion to some American businesses, and government issues of tax revenue.

What some economic and business expansion values consist of with certain computer and communication businesses is that various companies are competing over these distinct customers needing or wanting advanced technology. Microsoft and Apple for the last 2 decades have occasionally sold hundreds of thousands of products weekly, and sometimes daily. Apple Inc. CEO Tim Cook, and their Board Chairman Arthur Levinson have had to make decisions on massive products, and how to control the company which usually has a high costing premium for their stock. Contrary to Apple's stock price at well over $375.00 a share Microsoft has a slightly different concentration of expensive products. Their main business at Microsoft being Windows software, and then products like Xbox, with a few other items have had helpful sales with a stock price of around $35.00 dollars a share. This has appropriated business, and government tax revenue to an ailing U.S. economy.

As new products, and tax revenue applies to American industry Microsoft, and Apple have been somewhat competitors that have helped the U.S. economy. Some people like Donald Trump would slightly explain different, due to companies like GE, and more so Apple that manufacture heavily outside of the United States. This level of business activity with technology, and revenue conditionally advances in various regions. The most resourceful and detailed technology region is the Silicon Valley in California which is a bright spot of advancements within industry, and more so computer technology businesses of prosperity. Advancements in technology throughout America have also prospered in worldwide markets, but these have been conflicting issues to the overall American resources of business, and subjects that occasionally help the infrastructure.

Contrary to the weakness of the American infrastructure, the shift of computer science products with some disciplines of engineering has become a factual concern. This is valued with the market controlling subject of various internet companies like Amazon.com Inc, Google, and somewhat Facebook. Apart from more engineering, and construction projects, certain companies like Amazon with their CEO Jeff Bezos has also made billions of dollars in these newly established markets in the early 1990s, but the American economy is still far behind. Then during 2013 he made a decision to buy out the Washington Post newspaper for $250 million dollars which outlined how this industry has taken control of certain diversified markets.

Contrary to the Washington Post becoming a bargain buyout newspaper that has endured suffering, the Chicago Sun Times, and the Chicago Tribune were taken over at a low price. The variation of other newspaper companies like Knight Rider, Mercury News, Miami Herald, the Philadelphia Inquirer, and a few others have suffered similar negative changes due to the internet communication expansion. Therefore this, highly circulated level of daily products have been a transition to the economy from technology, and logical or local newspaper readership values that are facing a tremendous recovery effort.

Considering the digital age (c/o media) today certain heavy industry jobs, and businesses have become slightly quiet, or they are lacking a level of productive values to citizens as it applies to certain parts of the infrastructure. The format of the infrastructure has been a losing factor for people, and professionals that have lost ground, and assets on these vital business resources, and even expansion concerns. In this concern new, and old values of technology became an issue of balance throughout the profession of engineering, and the best solutions of their occasional performance in most aging city or town infrastructures. Then this becomes the management values of what will restructure the logic of economic business values in these aging cities or regions with mostly black Americans, and other minority citizens.

A major concern also can be observed with too much labor union activity, and not enough "management and professional minded" people that can create resourceful businesses. This has been the case with cities such as Detroit, Mi, Gary, In, Harrisburg, Pa, and now somewhat Chicago, Il which them and others have suffered severe economic hardships. Besides losing people to violent crime which is part of a severe expense, and closing schools these cities within conditional government have obligations to people's retirement pension funds which are being considered for reduced funding. Therefore as small businesses cannot expand, and crime, consist of an additional cost, the people in some concerns will continue to go backwards as a dysfunctional society. From here economic stability will not be established until social values are maintained in a lawful way.

Contrary to Detroit being the largest U.S. city to file for bankruptcy, other cities like Stockton, and San Bernardino, California have been hit hard before their bankruptcy filings. This also includes Jefferson County, Alabama whom, have filed bankruptcy lately observing a vast amount of cities, and regions having slightly similar economic problems. Stockton, California had 3 major problems that consisted of numerous city employees making close to $200,000.00 a year, and in 2007 they lead the United States in foreclosures which also included a concentration of bad or violent crime. This being a city south of Sacramento (the capital of California) both cities consisted of similar issues during the 2007 economic crisis. Therefore the concept of business expansion in America with government regulatory disciplines including logical enforcement of laws will play a vital role in the economic level of restructuring of the nation's economy.

Monopolies that control local markets like within Detroit, and other major inter-city concerns have suffered from households, and some businesses that for various economic reasons have gotten far behind on their utility bills. Detroit Edison which is now named DTE Energy Co has its headquarters in Detroit serving Southeastern Michigan, and some nationwide business matters. As they have over 10,000 employees in 2012 their CEO Gerard Anderson has been part of them making complex earnings. These earnings come from numerous households, schools, the auto industry, professional sporting events, and various agriculture based businesses similar to Kellogg in Battle Creek Michigan.

Apart from the difficulties of local citizens, and some businesses the City & County in Detroit has complex problems to solve. This is factual considering Detroit in 2013 has 78,000 abandon properties which is a loss of utility customers that becomes part of their good, and bad estimated utility company earnings. Then this becomes a difficult equation for their income earnings that pays for their overall business operation. Considering this observation a vast amount of restructuring must go on before this city, it's citizens, and certain businesses fully recovers.

Understanding major cities that have loss "tens of thousands" of citizens, and some with a decreasing population has caused an effect to the schools, and other government concerns of prosperity. One of the major results is that local and or regional government tax revenue losses occur, and restructuring values become vital issues. Then this hurts regulated monopolized utility companies (c/o then raising rates) which include other business concerns like banks with fewer customers then utility companies appropriating income from loans. This becomes the equation of homeownership "VS" public utility cost, but household income is still a vital factor. Therefore the combination of diversified monopolies has tremendously been observed which even includes numerous businesses, and the American newspaper industry taking the hardest hits. Their business losses have been in the millions of subscribed customers nationwide that is not an easy subject to digest.

The tremendous U.S. economy with various problems also includes the changing times of technology, and the factual conflict that there is not enough economic and social stability. This also becomes part of low income earning American people being angry or misguided as it applies to separate earnings not being managed or invested good enough to go around to numerous citizens. Along with various newspaper companies suffering, Eastman Kodak has filed for bankruptcy due to other companies expanding with digital cameras with very few, if any film products. The losing concept of the film business has given them at Eastman Kodak Co a severe problem within surviving in this slightly obsolete resource of a market. Therefore even the format of some taxable obligations has been eliminated from an important government equation, "contrary to bad corporate business" which has caused more citizens, and government employees to suffer.

Observing the U.S. economy, and the changing industry times in America, various markets and monopolized businesses consist of entities which require a stable banking industry. Banking is a factor that most all businesses and households depend on for financial, and or economic resources of business managing disciplines. Also this is part of an important business network to manage responsible conditions of money in a diversified capacity. Then the Federal Reserve Bank and their 2012 Chairman Ben Bernanke have taken observation of various economic issues that have made "business, and finance" a crisis which American banking lately must restructure its own business activity. This becomes a logical factor to understand the format of a productive money circulation within the managing, and regulating of member banks in America upon which all require a level of stability.

Contrary to the Federal Reserve Bank the 2000 to 2007 economic crisis also consisted of Fannie Mae, and Freddie Mac suffering to the near extent of temporary insolvency. This was before their equity relief of being bailout for $187 billion dollars occurred. Then the mortgage, credit, and debt crisis took away numerous small and large business earning's, and utility company income when citizens suffered through various overwhelming problems. These problems included massive foreclosures during a period of failing banks.

Wachovia with their CEO Kennedy Thompson suffered negative write-downs and losses after their purchase of Golden West bank. This crisis was also during a housing boom, and then another crisis of collateralized debt obligations from mortgage backed securities gone, bad. Wachovia failed to recognize this issue with Golden West bank whom had numerous bad loans on their books. Therefore similar banks like Indy Mac just to name a few consisted of severe financial problems that caused harm to the American economy.

As a certain amount of financial problems started, during the tenure of Federal Reserve Chairman Alan Greenspan hundreds of banks suffered from bad loans. During the time and appointment of Chairman Ben Bernanke Wachovia bank had bought out numerous smaller banks with bad loans. Years soon after this; Wachovia was on its way out of business (c/o bankruptcy) to be bought out by Wells Fargo. This consisted of some supervision from the Federal Deposit Insurance Corporation with Chairperson Sheila Bair, and President George Bush. Understanding this concept of events the important decision was to increase the guaranteed insured deposit level of bank funds from $100,000.00 to $250,000.00.

Contrary to monopolies the stability of the U.S. economy has endured survival from the executive branch, and the legislative branch of American government with vital decisions of importance not seen since the 1920s, and the 1930s. The Judicial branch of the American system of government was tagged with the concern that they must be more logical with decisions for smaller businesses that suffered from anti-trust legal issue of discipline. These are concerns that can advance smaller businesses to a level of prosperous growth in business, and even government stability with expansion. From this factual observation of executive, legislative, and judicial concerns the U.S. government with the Federal Deposit Insurance Corporation (FDIC) has only raised the "insured deposit" level 3 times since the 1930s. This FDIC issue started from $12,500.00 in the 1930s, then, was raised to $100,000.00 in the 1980s, and now during 2008 it was established at $250,000.00 to support bank deposits after this recent 2007 economic crisis.

Considering the times following the 1930s various economic security law values had been established. These factual conditions of programs such as Social Security, Workmen's Compensation, labor union concerns, and a few other governed details have stabilized the American peoples financial, and economic resources. Even now today with various government values of economic stabilization the American economy in 2007 recognized its worse recession, and failed with numerous citizens financially misguided. Therefore with a century of government changes when tuff economic times occur, certain retirement concerns for Americans, and or disable citizens (c/o employment) can have adequate income. This funding from the U.S. government is for various expenses, and logical spending that has been considered appropriate for normal living standards.

Now from the year 2010 to 2013 enormous amounts of corporate and government employee pension plan benefits are being considered for reduced funding, and value, if not eliminated. Then agencies like the U.S. Government's Pension Benefit Guaranty Corporation have been helpful, but this factor of government is now being forced to pay out more money for failed corporate and government pension plans. Understanding this agency during the first decade of 2000 the vast amount of banks, and corporate businesses that have failed with long term commitments to employees becomes a logical condition outside of a bankruptcy filing. Then as Americans observe the billions of dollars that were committed to employee retirements the condition of good, bad or excellent management disciplines become a recognized value of importance.

As it applies to various monopolies that were bought out by corporate businesses like Enron, the utility Portland General Electric had various employees whom loss tremendous amounts of public utility company managed money. This monopolized business buy out like so many others was a severe problem to a large amount of long term employees, and corporate businesses who's valued earnings, and liquidity where dissolved. Portland GE like numerous other utility companies has tens of thousands plus steady customers, and resourceful income with stable liquidity. Therefore this made them and other utility businesses interesting for corporate activities of a controlling interest within liquefied investments.

The mixture between corporate businesses, government, and public utility monopolies in the late 1990s, and early 2000s has been part of complex greed with the leverage of utility company assets. Within the factor of leveraging assets that exist from a utility company this is where a few people become very wealthy, and then the people as consumers, and utility workers occasionally suffered. Understanding this during the 1990s, and the 1st decade of 2000 most massive financial crimes have been committed surrounding utility companies. Observing these types of crimes, and complex investments like private equity, and more hedge funds American small or retired investors most times loss severely. Then contrary to public utility monopolies, the concept of banking and insurance such as with AIG, and a vast amount of others have created a market of severe instability.

Almost every electric public utility has changed by now having a parent company along with some communication companies with conflicting activities. Besides WorldCom, and Enron numerous utility companies that had or offered investment opportunities have become part of a smoke screen by parent company holdings, or business conflicting issues. Then as numerous bank ownership issues have changed the American insurance industry has more so moved into the business of investments, and commerce banking which has slightly taking the citizens of the United States back to the 1920s era of economics.

CHAPTER ELEVEN

The Most Complex Monopolies Of Today

An American Study Of Business & Monopolies

The Most Complex Monopolies Of Today

To understand the most complex monopolies in American business today during 2013 is somewhat similar to the last 100 years with more advanced products, and various business ventures. Even more so this is part of observing the workable conditions, and resources of the United States government which regulates large, and some small business operations. Therefore as various monopoly, or conglomerate businesses operate, or control markets, it becomes complex how they invest, and divest with numerous issues of successful or conditional patents.

What has made various monopolies an issue of control is their intellectual rights of ownership within products, extensive industrial operations, and or valid services. Also the level of responsible, and lawful business activities with decisions from employees (c/o some labor unions), and management are important factors of prosperous business. This becomes vital upon understanding that people need, or find a logical use for these monopolized products or services that usually consist of chemicals, electronics, or mechanical technology products. Upon this observation the people's daily condition of household living, or business values usually can change, or be maintained for the better of professional services and hopefully not the worse for the people, business, and or even government. This has been observed with President Obama's internet applications for the Affordable Care Act with massive people and insurance companies as an over sight.

Observing various markets the concept of railroad, pharmaceutical, chemicals, and shipbuilding companies are a few industries where monopolized business operations can occur with advanced equipment. These are businesses like Ely Lilly, Pfizer Inc, Norfork Southern, Union Pacific, Amtrak, General Dynamics, and others that hold strong economic values. This is relevant of how they endure conflicts along with positive sales similar to utility companies that may be involved in wireless technology, nuclear technology, and or alternative energy advancements. Considering these diversified industries the cost of their products or services can have good, bad, or negative effects which can cause diversified concerns to the American society of people.

Recently nuclear submarines and battle ships for the U.S. Navy have been part of highly regulated and advanced markets. Northrop Grumman Shipbuilding and their management understand this level of monopolized advancements within U.S. Defense products will be a subject protected under the U.S. Department of Defense legal disciplines such as the Berry Amendment. The Berry Amendment within laws holds preference for American defense products. This understanding is similar to U.S. Department of Defense drones, and the Patriot Missile System developed and manufactured by Raytheon Corporation with other defense products.

Understanding various issues of business advancements the company that establishes the first or numerous patents on various products usually last 2, 3, or more years if not forever with the lawful rights of these products. This is relevant with concerns of defense or non-defense related products as a controlling monopoly in a market. Therefore with good business skills, contrary to government activity these businesses establish good economic value, and social conditions that are observed throughout America.

Contrary to Americas market of advanced products that only one, or a few companies produce, the legal and monopolized condition of business has become a major concern of resources. Then apart from record amounts of civil violations of law, and fraud recently surrounding various utility companies, some advancements of technology in America has been prosperous, and helpful. Actually the problem of WorldCom, Enron, Ameritech, and a few others caused a setback for the numerous companies that they bought out, or which caused a conflict to advance their levels of business liquidity. In retrospect these businesses that controlled certain markets with fraudulent or unlawful activities destroyed the liquidity of numerous American citizens which included some bad decisions from government.

Understanding the concept of monopolies today have become occasionally more complex to find as competitors that are making an effort to keep up the issue of economic, and patent law issues of stability. This is still difficult for a vast amount of citizens of the United States who need opportunities, besides hedge fund, and private equity investors that are taking a large part of these competitive business investment earnings. These investors are important, but even more so financial institutions caused inefficiency to certain mutual fund investors during the late 1990s. This concern for small investors is an issue which must be restored for small prosperous investors to grow without trading interruptions. The only other major economic conflict that prevails is that utilities are a working force in America, and how this conflict consist of some other monopolized products are in mass production within other countries. Then this has been a tremendous loss to the economy, American citizens, and more so workers.

Besides every public utility company, various railroad companies, and companies like Microsoft Corp, and Apple Inc has existed with the concept of a monopolized business with tremendous products, and various responsibilities. Microsoft has been one of the major issues of complex U.S. Anti-Trust laws which has inter-phased with computers becoming user friendly. Also this included their conflicting and slightly inappropriate market control of internet purchasing power surrounding this powerful, and arbitrary communication and computer programming network of businesses. As both Microsoft, and Apple Inc work with all communication companies (c/o AT&T, Comcast, and Verizon), they consist of technology agreements that appropriate internet, wired, and wireless communication networks. Therefore as old and new technology come together the format of people as individual citizens, and business owners must stay alert.

The Federal Communication Commission (FCC) has been a vital part of lawfully consolidating America's resource of wired and wireless communication networks. Contrary to the FCC's duties with radio, and television the lawful arbitration of communication utility systems even includes the internet with issues in the United States that need to be governed appropriately. Understanding this a large array of problems from the internet, and other industries have expanded into an uncontrollable force causing conflict which need better legislature, and court room issue of liability. Therefore being alert is an issue for millions of people and their resources of concern to understand when something is unlawfully wrong.

A strong level of being alert, in this internet communication bubble, and or issue of technology expansion have consisted of government (c/o the U.S. Department of Justice) with various citizens, and Microsoft competitors. As Bill Gates testified in a legal case filed by 18 state governments, the U.S. Dept. of Justice, and the District of Columbia in 2 separate filings had changed business at Microsoft which was ordered through a "Consent Decree". The consent decree changed some of the visible internet activity of Microsoft advertising, and their sales on the internet against businesses like Netscape Communication Corporation. This also vitally included their competitive issues over the browser technology that helps a computers cursor move around a monitor, and click onto various programmable icons. Then this became important to overcome with any destructive issues that technology may offer. This was a factual logic which may cause problems to the people, sometimes their secured assets, and the anti-trust equality of other "internet and or corporate businesses".

Managing secured assets of the American people, most businesses, and some worldwide markets during the 1st decade of 2000 has been a factor of good and bad people that occasionally don't care for the laws of the U.S. Constitution. Even a vast amount of lawyers don't argue these issues easily, and therefore victims may be considered ignorant until an enormous amount of people's money, or their life savings have been loss. Observing this the best businesspeople, and their customers or cliental usually have a careful way of doing business. Contrary to some argumentative, and government regulative issues, one of the more complex responsibilities of a monopoly is to occasionally divest corporate assets. These are divisions or subsidiaries of corporations upon which by law requirements from court proceedings, and or the U.S. Department of Justice they have requirements to react, and regroup.

Apart from businesses whom divested certain assets like American Telephone & Telegraph Corp, and Standard Oil Company, the business operation at Monsanto Company Inc have divested with conflicts. Monsanto has had enormous dealings with various state governments, and more so the U.S. federal courts as plaintiffs, and defendants. Monsanto with their present CEO Hugh Grant has endured complex issues as the leading manufacture, and patent holder of genetically engineered farming seeds, and herbicide "weed killing" glyphosate. This herbicide is under the brand name Roundup which is used by a large group of farmers along with Monsanto, and some of their subsidiary manufactured or chemically refined products. Understanding this, even the workers at Monsanto have high levels of responsible handling of these products so that they are not infected, or injured during production.

Between Monsanto, the United States Department of Agriculture (USDA), and the U.S. Patent office "together", they have worked for decades to improve inventions, products for farming, and the health of crops for consumption by people. This working process has become important with issues of concern for the American people, farmers, and government. Considering these factors this included issues within business transactions which have become part of developing a farmer's soil, various food crop developments, and their system of food processing.

A certain amount of farmers worried that patent infringement lawsuits would be filed by Monsanto against them if additional or conflicting patents or negligence became an issue. This consisted of Monsanto's genetically engineered seeds may have been used improperly, and then how it may contaminate the soil upon which the farmers had a mixture of seeds, water, and or chemicals. Therefore the technical process of farming even as the weather plays a vital role the USDA and how farmers used certain products became important with technical details every year concerning the outcome of their harvest.

Contrary to the mixture of herbicide and seeds various conflicts which are based on evaluations between the Monsanto Company, and certain traditional farming with some experts became complex issues that could cause ether side as individual businesses to fail. The logic of this process of farming is mixed between herbicide glyphosate (basically an unwanted weed killer) occasionally was considered not always 100% productive. This has sometimes cost farmers money whom, have multiple or massive acres of land, and these chemicals occasionally made a portion of their crops suffer. Contrary to these factors the condition of growing crops every year had numerous, risk that appropriately needed these Monsanto products along with irrigation, and prefect weather.

Monsanto Company Inc, and corporate businesses like Deere & Company (c/o John Deere machinery) are important businesses that most farmers depend on to conduct their seasonal, and diversified process of planting, growing, and the harvesting of crops. If you compare Monsanto, Deere & Company, and a few other corporate businesses that cater to farmers, "Monsanto" has endured more legal action filings then a vast amount of others. One of the most recent international debates with Monsanto did not consist of tremendous legal arguments, but caused severe protest in Germany, and throughout the United Kingdom. The protest was over a "patent application and business practice" on pig breeding techniques. Therefore, in 2007 Monsanto Co Inc divested with the sale of Monsanto Choice Genetics to Newsham Genetics LC located in West Des Moines, Iowa ending their patent work within the business of pig breeding, and any associated patents.

As it applies to American farmers Deere & Company has provided helpful John Deere tractors, and other mechanical products since the 1800s to the farming industry. Their agriculture products, and market value have advanced with other major corporate businesses, but with somewhat more satisfied farming, construction, and landscaping customers. Observing 2012 Deere & Company has maintained being the largest manufacture of agriculture machinery in America, and worldwide with annual income recently over $3.5 billion dollars. The appreciation of John Deere equipment even with their control of certain markets is an economic plus to the American economy, and various "light and heavy" equipment industry concerns. Therefore Deere & Company with their headquarters in Moline, Illinois which includes a vast array of machinery products is not a complex monopoly, but their stable resource of business in America is astute, and helpful.

To regain observation of monopolies in America the issue of various public utility companies has changed with the times in conflicting ways. These issues start with the Public Utility Holding Company Act (PUHCA) with the first legislative version starting in 1935, and the most recent version during 2008. The concept of divesture was considered vital in the 1930s with the PUCHA legislature which was also considered the Wheeler-Rayburn Act that kept most public utility holding companies in separate states with appropriate regulation. This was mostly for electric (c/o some gas) utilities such as numerous Edison Company franchises making them single integrated units serving limited customers in certain geographical regions.

The difference between the 1930s, and the first decade of 2000 with regional electric, and gas public utility companies is that

"Trust-Busting" and Investor securities regulation consisted of economic and engineering stability values of discipline. Contrary to Tennessee Valley Authority being government owned various other regional electric, and gas public utilities have been reestablished to a level of corporate control. Duke Energy Corporation has been slightly different as a holding company with various Articles of Incorporation in the state of North Carolina. Other businesses such as within Exelon Corporation, FirstEnergy Corporation, and Entergy Corporation have expanded regional monopoly control, and are slightly different from the formal Public Utility Holding Company Act of 1935. This requirement of the 1935 Act held most public utilities in individual state borders with professional levels of discipline.

In review of various public utilities and the establishment of the U.S. Department of Energy in 1977 most professional and legal issues have slightly been rearranged. This includes three issues between government, and business that are relevant with public utility companies with some financial, and economic concerns having become a conflict. As financial institutions have taken more interest in public utility company investments they have also taken a certain level of the profitable earnings. Those discretionary issues are the mix between Articles of Incorporation, the definition of Corporation, and the lawful disciplines of the Public Utility Company Holding Act— "past and now present".

One commission becoming more active with the PUCHA established issues is the Federal Energy Regulatory Commission. Observing the Federal Energy Regulatory Commission they now consist of a limited role in cost allocations for multi-state utility holding companies as this commission replaced the Federal Power Commission in the late 1970s. Enron Corporation led the conflicting way before the PUCHA of 2005 Act was passed in these multi-state monopolizing utility industry concerns along with WorldCom. These changes with utility business values, was also slightly different then Exelon, FirstEnergy, and Entergy. Understanding this they have been slightly conditional with corporate issues apart from traditional "Edison" holding companies for one state region's. Duke Energy also is different by being more detailed in the 6 states that they serve with somewhat over 7 million customers during the first decade of 2000.

These changes or additions in the public utility industry become important in the profession of engineering contrary to economic issues with investment banking, various state laws, and issues of the U.S. Environmental Protection Agency, the U.S. Patent office, and other concerns. Advancements in technology or newly developed chemicals require amendments or additional legislature to be certain that the American society is safe. Also as certain utility companies have become multi-state operations some state laws that are different from state to state are part of their resourceful obligation of liability. As they gained more financial control, the conflict of interest in these newly developed public utility company concerns was partly an issue that led to the boycott of the American financial markets in 2009, and 2010. Therefore with the good, and more so bad issues of U.S. legislative repeals the banking industry, the utilities industry, investment banking and a few others (c/o a mortgage crisis) have consisted of conflicts that are hard for the American people to except economically.

Within the most complex part of American business regional monopolies which includes the stability of economics, engineering, and business with Articles of Incorporation have been a reestablished concern similar to the 1930s. These are issues with some damages that have slightly over-thrown the Public Utility Company Holding Act, and its common law values for the American society. The repeal of the Glass Steagall Act seems to be a similar problem in the banking industry. Therefore, careful decisions within the American system of governed legislature, and the courts must be astute, honorable to the people, and be workable for the people.

These resources are the format of how Exelon Corporation, FirstEnergy Corporation, and Entergy Corporation have become companies which are part of a multi-billion market of monopolized regional businesses. They also become aggressive with some conditions of greed or advancements of liquidity. In the 1970s, 80s, and early 1990s public utility holding companies such as Commonwealth Edison of Chicago consisted of multiple common and preferred stock prices which changed after Exelon Corporation created them as a subsidiary. In the neighboring state of Indiana, the Northern Indiana Public Service Company (NIPSCO) became a subsidiary of Nisource. This business trend created "complex" investments, professional standards, and some opportunities for various people and small investors. Also this then provided more control to hedge funds, and private equity investors which surly put small investors at a disadvantage.

As these monopolizing businesses changed with diversified control, the market of hiring people with economic disciplines or investor control became an issue. The societal factor of crime, and a mortgage crisis also became some of the other major issues of how the American economy during the 1st decade of 2000 changed various public utility industry concerns. With less people working and people having household economic stability the issue of public utility companies raising their rates became a tremendous conflict. This economic adjustment, consist of conditional customer arguments, but the employees, and stock holders were also a part of this equation of events. Therefore even as this included American and sometimes foreign investors the United States Public Utility Holding Company Act became slightly un-American with utility companies "wanting more money" with "less customers". This is factual unless they are making major utility upgrades that are helpful.

Duke Energy Corporation being the largest electric power holding company in the United States has achieved progress in various ways. Their progress with ups, and downs in electrical power distribution, and more so nuclear energy have been expensive with resourceful distribution. Also this includes alternative energy with wind farms, solar energy, and conditionally nuclear energy that consist of an expensive cost. Then these become legislative matters of laws, and conditions that are formatted with regulators from the American system of government. Observing Duke Energy, and their recent CEO Lynn Good, they have worked hard for almost a decade on a newly built nuclear energy plant in South Carolina. This project to be built in Cherokee County, SC is a joint business agreement between Duke Power, and the Southern Company which includes equipment from Westinghouse Electric Company.

Observing the extensive cost of a nuclear energy plant by Duke Energy Corporation becomes a value as they are spending a $160 million dollars on this South Carolina project which started after 2009 as a massive commitment. Also part of this commitment will consist of long term financial involvement in the plant at between $5 to $6 billion dollars. Then this also includes Westinghouse nuclear energy equipment that is observed as pressurized water nuclear reactors. Therefore out of the hundreds of electric utility companies that have considered investing in the engineering, equipment, and construction of a nuclear energy plant financial and argumentative issues have been apparent. This mostly becomes the logic between "coal VS nuclear" electric energy utility business resources. Observing these factors as energy, and public utility issues the American society has established a resource of additional technology that most times is only managed by a monopolized business.

CHAPTER TWELVE

The Constitution & The Internet

An American Study Of Business & Monopolies

The Constitution & The Internet

The internet is not "truly" a monopoly, but it is a major resource of monopolized discipline. Observing the United States Constitution and the arbitrary "network or infrastructure" of the internet becomes an issue of at least four factors contrary to unlawful computer hackers. Those factors are good, bad, evil, and conflicting networks that occasionally appropriate access to people that don't care for a lawful society of conditional liability, and sometimes even "U.S. or worldwide National Security". As valid as these advancements in technology are, this has made computers a pivotal resource for expanded information, but it is still a concern with the 4th Amendment, and other amendments of the U.S. Constitution.

The U.S. Constitution has been known to Grant Power, Limit Power, and Protect Against the Abuse of Power. These issues have been valued on the bases that even an American citizen doing banking, sending email letters, and or conducting other business transactions online are a subject of new laws, or legislative concerns. This technology with the internet and satellites is most times faster than other correspondence, but unlawful activities can cause a loss of peoples conditional resource of documented liability, financial resources, or in some cases their reputation. Then this has become one of the issues of fairness which most times apply to the 1st and 4th Amendments of the U.S. Constitution.

Understanding recent legal conditions within the "Freedom" of Religion and Speech laws along with the U.S. Rights of Confidentiality upon Affirmation have become severely violated with the likes of conditional bullies. These issues are similar to "Man VS Machinery", "Man VS Chemical Weapons", or even "Man VS Satellites" as a monopolizing system. Then as the American society along with other countries observes U.S. Anti-Trust laws, and enormous issues of business to conduct, more values of "Constitutional Liability" become important within the use of the internet with its regulatory values. Considering these issues the internet bubble with advancements in satellite technology has pushed some economic levels of security full speed backwards in the American society.

Since the U.S. Constitution was established in the late 1700s various conditions of the American society including numerous industries have changed, and then the laws had reason to be amended, and or adjusted. These are diversified resources of the progress that have given some American businesses advancements within certain computer operations, internet advertising, and various means of communication with an expanded virtue. This virtual reality is due to diversified opinions, and certain conditions of liability considering sometimes the level of activity has become similar to conflicting video games. Understanding this various video games and reality has come to close for the valid understanding of Constitutional Liability.

As massive transactions and exchanges are made on the World Wide Web (www) this concentration of major monopolizing activity is broad. This is based on millions of people, businesses, organizations, and even government having made investments in these network disciplines of good, and bad business, and or social activities. Considering this it must be recognized that individual citizens now hold some monopoly powers, but the question is can the masses of diversified people keep lawful control, order, or discipline? This is due to the fact that these tools of extensive and sometimes unauthorized networking have values of technology which can be irresponsibly destructive. Contrary to these issues a vast amount of people do share certain documents, and pitchers of value, and or decency which is most times a constructive level of networking.

The laws of Social Media that exist for people with expanded networks of information technology are totally different from the way most newspaper companies make an effort to honor, and comply with the 1st Amendment of the U.S. Constitution. The news media is a professional resource apart from some unprofessional issues of social media upon which laws are more commonly considered in the resourceful business of providing Americans with news stories. Therefore besides the best internet activities the concept of humiliation, and destructive activities of conditional, or excessive harm is not completely abusive with power that eliminates the Constitution's meaning of Domestic Tranquility.

Most investments by the United States government, and various corporate businesses have come with a conflicting price as some information sharing of classified and non-classified documents have been part of potential harm. Very few of these issues have been argued in the U.S. Supreme Court, but certain U.S. federal district courts have taken on discretionary arguments like who might be the true inventor of Facebook apart from Mark Zuckerberg. This usually occurs when products or services are successful, and conflicting issues occur, or even dangerous information is provided to certain people which becomes threatening to hundreds, or thousands of people or more. Then this is the fact of how America, and various parts of the world have had radical, and dangerous people gain support from large, and closely monopolizing groups of people.

Some groups of monopolizing bad people have been a tremendous harm. These are people like Osama bin Laden (al-Qaeda), Jean-Paul Akayesu (Rwanda), Foday Sankoh (Sierra Leone), Slobodan Milosevic (Serbia / Yugoslavia) observing those who caused mutilation, and massive terror against certain innocent people. Also some Americans that supported an enemy foreign agenda, gang activity, and or violent attacks like with the Columbine High School massacre in the state of Colorado has increased in other well developed states in America. Then this seems to be part of unregulated new technology which is appropriating the worse crimes by various people. This 1999 Columbine disaster, and attack by Eric Harris, and Dylan Klebold whom both committed suicide was also a conflicting part of them becoming very active with discretionary internet activity.

During the Columbine High School massacre the 2 youthful gunmen killed 12 students, and a teacher with more than 20 others in the school injured from the shooting. Also as these have become violent and ruthless attacks of crime and concern with bi-lateral resources of destructive behavior, Americans suffered in various regions. Then vital concerns lingered with these young people's exposure, and output of social media messages, and opinions. This has led to the good, and bad of information technology that has been tremendous with conflicting support, or isolated vigilance. Therefore this means that the Federal Communication Commission (FCC) should have had better procedures with the Federal Bureau of Investigation (FBI) to recognize creditable threats to America, and or U.S. National Security.

Another unobserved threat to America was the information gathering result of people like Mohamed Atta as the leader of the 9-11

Report terrorist attacks working with Osama bin Laden, and others. It was crucial upon how he gained valued information about vital issues in America which escalated some conditions for terrorism in the United States approaching the September 11th attacks of 2001. As these issues of National Security where not observed properly, or even taken serious these people from the Middle East have created a network that in 2013 is still an occasional threat to the American society. Therefore in the 1970s, the 1980s, and the 1990s the concept of hijacking U.S. commercial airplanes was taken to new and disastrous levels.

As more American's, and people from other countries explore the infrastructure use of the internet with companies like Facebook, Twitter, Google, YouTube, and Yahoo the good, and bad resources of communication, and social networking control becomes a vital observation. This is relevant upon when the U.S. government equation of the Federal Communication Commission regulative involvement, and the American system of government has more enforcement (c/o the Government Performance & Results Act) recommended duties. Observing these factors consist of the outrageous amount of crime, exploitation, conspiracies, and even madness which some people engaged in with social media web sites. Contrary to legislative adjustments and enforcement these become critical issues. In retrospect more people, government, and businesses have taken responsible advantage of internet web site advertising, and this is valuable to an enormous amount of business software operating applications which have been appropriately activated.

The communication factors of advancement here was occasionally discussed with broadband issues of technology upon which even Enron Corporation became active with upon offering their conflicting services. To clearly understand various corporate businesses that offer services like broadband which is a fairly new technology, "a company" has to be Constitutionally Liable. This was far from the case of WorldCom, Enron, and even Ameritech Corp which held some different concerns apart from AT&T with wireless communication, internet, and other advanced issues of communication technology. Understanding this Verizon, Comcast, and AT&T have been the more stable corporate businesses to offer broadband (c/o internet services) to the American general public with "somewhat" logical understanding, and approval from the FCC.

Observing the U.S. Constitution during the 1st decade of 2000 the Federal Communication Commission and all communication corporate businesses with expanded technology became part of certain goals that had to be identified as important. The FCC identified these issues as Broadband, Competition, Spectrum, Media, Public Safety "with" Homeland Security, and Modernizing a resourceful level of the FCC's operation. Considering this, the U.S. government's Office of Management and Budget was appropriated in a direction from the U.S. Congress and the President with the Government Performance Results Act of 1993 which was part of overall strategic plans, and reports. This legislative act after the first Persian Gulf War in the early 1990s affected almost everything the U.S. government could not easily correct "except" certain necessities like delivering mail.

Understanding these identified communication issues, the FCC's former Chairman's of William Kennard, and Michael Powell became pivotal government officials with extensive communication technology reviews. This was during the increase of networking computers, and wireless communication which included the subjects of expanded internet, and cell phone technology. Those years from 1991 to 2006 included Kevin Martin, and then Julius Genachowski during a few years after the internet bubble burst with certain businesses failing "apart from some successful" ambition. This consisted of almost 90% of America's network of computers, and wireless communication infrastructure systems being expanded, and upgraded. Therefore the commitment of all five "FCC" commissioners during the 1st decade of 2000 became critical for them to keep up with the changing conditions of networking communication technology which also applied to the U.S. Constitution.

As corporate business operations expand in non-monopolizing, and some slightly monopolized controlling markets for computers, the internet, cell phones, and other devices consisted of certain industry standards and legislature that are still being constitutionally considered. These matters consisted of major factors from complacent American government consisting of keeping up with technology advancements. This was also observed during the increase in terrorist threats against America, and others with a very intense war in Iraq, and Afghanistan which became a conflicting factor.

In retrospect the United States has still kept a strong hand on developing technology that is relevant for defense, and other civil service purposes. These critical factors were apparent even understanding that President Barack Obama had eliminated a majority of the budget for the National Aeronautics and Space Administration (NASA) from certain space travel, and technology developments. Then a certain amount of research and development has also kept a concentration of developing products as a strategic subject of positive diversion from the U.S. Constitution's liability of American domestic use and advancements. Basically the United States like a few other countries has technological products that they are not to use against their own citizens.

Understanding the American society and other well developed countries advancing with the same technology has put places like England, and the U.S. (c/o New York, Virginia, Ohio, and other states affected by the 9-11 attacks) in a vulnerable position. The concept of this with "enemy or terrorizing nations" using some of the same technology has also penetrated the security of these and other well developed countries. This becomes the major factor of over sight technology upon which Americans have more concerns to address with government redress. Also other bad nations may work to destroy the U.S. while Americans are rightfully occupied, but government has a duty for this concern. Theoretically the concept of "developing nations" has somewhat been tremendously delayed apart from terrorizing countries, or similar issues like the many natural disasters observed in the recent 2011 earthquake with a tsunami in Japan, and tropical storm Sandy on the east coast of the United States.

A monopolizing issue of destruction has been considered with the recent social networking of activity in most Muslim regions of the Middle East, and North Africa. This is a recent factor of will these countries ever rebuild where people can live in homes apart from the many facilities that have been destroyed in war time conflicts. Therefore as more countries have been inducted into the United Nations, and a few have been expelled with tremendous issues of violence, some technology can still be a security threat. These have been issues applicable to U.S. and International Security Counsel, observing matters which are vital concerns to be recognized.

Developing countries with monopolizing businesses are part of an issue that a lawful equation may be needed for the equality of all hard working people. Various countries that are slightly divided like Africa and parts of the Middle East which are using some forms of technology to increase their resources of terrorizing conflicts have implemented slightly unreliable conditions of government or parliamentary leadership. Considering this, various dictators have led some countries into some of their worse times in life and history. Then businesses that monopolize in those countries are more prone to be part of dictatorships that hold a vast amount of people back. Understanding this in the United States the "Separation of Powers" in government for, and by the people has given more citizens, and businesses an opportunity to create or improve products, and or services that consumers appreciate.

Every country since the 1970s that expanded with productive businesses have did so with the logic of their people peacefully working together as much as possible. This has been relevant contrary to the fact that there are rich and poor people that have to make decisions that are lawfully good for themselves, and others. As these issues apply to large businesses, and government leadership values of conditional subjects like the internet, this has become a tool, and social media value that must be controlled in lawful order. Social media throughout America has become an issue that has exceeded violations of the law that monopolizing newspapers, and journalist have violated occasionally for the last 100 years. This was their good, bad or indifference within obtaining a news story. Therefore how major news media corporations, and organizations conduct their business has been affected by the highest level of social networking with conflicting liability.

Traditional newspapers and the internet has become a strange issue of conflicting liability with financial concerns of indifference. During the 1990s, and the first decade of 2000 numerous newspaper companies have filed bankruptcy or have closed down their operation forever. Contrary to this fact there are still thousands of newspapers operating in America that have adjusted to these technological times of change. This has become the conflicting, and diversified issue of how the internet has lawfully put news printed papers in a complex position of vital economic restructuring.

The newspaper industry in America has consisted of business monopolizing strength since the 1700s with their changing technology, and resources of today. Now during the late 1990s and 2000 the internet, and printed newspapers have become conditional competitors moving towards partnerships. Most large and productive newspaper companies have changed with the times by becoming resourcefully active on the internet. Even the internet company Amazon.com founder Jeff Bezos has increased his wealth, and during August of 2013 he purchased the Washington Post for $250 million dollars. This was slightly different with Rupert Murdoch buying the Dow Jones Company (c/o the Wall Street Journal), and his experience of owning various newspaper companies. Therefore newspapers like the Wall Street Journal, the Washington Post, and a vast amount of others have kept their businesses alive contrary to industry wide economic conflicts or losses.

Understanding the 1000s of printed newspapers in America which usually monopolize in small, midsize, and large cities and towns throughout the United States the internet has become one of their more powerful, and or conditional tools. The internet has also become a competitive force against the U.S. Postal Service business matters during the 1st decade of 2000. These conflicts here consisted of more bill payments through the internet than postal service letters driving the earnings of stamp sales down. Then this becomes the resource of how the U.S. Postal Service has determined Saturday mail delivery services to be not cost effective with other major issues like closing post offices, and sorting centers.

The challenges of the U.S. Postal Service with their 2013 Postmaster General Patrick Donahoe started with a budget issue that includes a mandate of $5.5 billion dollars a year account to pre-fund retiree healthcare. Congress passed this legislature as the Postal Accountability and Enhancement Act in 2006. As the American economy soon after went into a recession in 2007 and 2008 the Postal Services budget became an economic deficit issue. This included them looking for other sources of revenue as the U.S. mortgage crisis effected them as well. Observing these factors the economic deficit and the American economy became part of numerous down falls to households and businesses which also included the good, and more so bad of some postal employees that could not appropriate better solutions.

Considering various issues, the U.S. Postal Service lost $15.9 billion dollars in 2012, and earned revenue of $65 billion dollars with extensive overhead cost similar to their competitors. As the internet has a high percentage of users along with the U.S. Constitution giving businesses and government enterprises the scale of logic, dependable businesses had to take additional resources serious. This fact is conflicting between the U.S. Postal Service, United Parcel Service, Federal Express Corporation and a few others that have not achieved strong, or monopolizing market control. All three entities hold strong within their liabilities, delivery services, internet service disciplines, and other business values, but the comparison is complex. This comparison consist of corporate and government resources that occasionally have good shareholders, board of directors, and or management issues that keep astute business operating values in order.

Apart from astute business issues the concept of government enterprise values that use to be publicly owned businesses have endured economic and financial struggles that need to be stabilized. Amtrak, who's core business values are not completely efficient with the internet have seem to suffer similar to the U.S. Postal Service when the economy is in conflicting shape. Sometimes this applies to Constitutional law concerns, and occasionally new technology that is not cost effective. Therefore Americans should be mindful that the internet and other industries will continue to change, but sometimes this will include critical court proceedings, and amendments to the U.S. Constitution. Then the people and business owners being astute for survival or prosperity may spread to various U.S. government operations that benefit the people.

CHAPTER THIRTEEN

Constitutional Law, Wireless Communication & Satellites

An American Study Of Business & Monopolies

Constitutional Law, Wireless Communication & Satellites

Observing most monopoly business operations and the United States Constitution there has been numerous technology developments with successful outcomes over the centuries. These technology changes, with advancements since the U.S. Constitutions, 1776 established signing into America's "central and supreme" law is part of what made America productive within becoming a well-developed country. Then these issues of development following the Revolutionary, and Civil wars consisted of monopolies like Western Union "Company" with Morse code in the 1930s. This and other technology developments took centuries of changes, but now during the first 2 decades of 2000 with technology violations of law the American system of legislature, and the judiciary have become a relevant issue in numerous critical matters.

The U.S. Separation of Powers has become a big, but common responsibility to the people, and their U.S. Constitutional Rights. These are Constitutional rights that should keep the people from becoming too angry with each other without war like conditions with the concern of executive, legislative, and judicial government duties. Technology within the internet, wireless communication, and satellites has been only conditionally observed as a problem during and slightly before the 1st decade of 2000 as a tremendous concern for additional regulation. Considering this fact with a conflicting American economy, some internet and overall legislature is vital to be though about, but this must be done at a resourceful rate before certain levels of damage become out of control.

As the U.S. Constitution is over 230 years old it has only been amended 27 times. None of these 27 amendments apply in wording to the use of good, bad, or Americas resource of complex and diversified technology. This can be recognized with amendments to slavery, taxes, congressional pay raises, voting, citizenship, and other issues that are lawfully outlined. Contrary to these important amendments over the last 100 years telecommunication, satellites, and even the conflicts of chemical weapons have only slightly become important constitutional issues.

Between wired and wireless communication, commercial satellites, and the least conflicting of all domestically in the U.S.—"chemical weapons", the time for improved Constitutional Liability with existing regulation is NOW! This has become, important within the many good, and then even more so bad or conflicting issues of crime and negligence that people occasionally suffer from with the arbitrary and new resources of technology. So therefore even as Articles were established in the U.S. Constitutional responsibilities of government, this is, and will be a format for government, professionals, and the people to work together.

Upon the factor of more people with conflicting anger, and the increase of people hearing voices seems to be a concern of how new health problems with sophisticated technology have occurred. The most sophisticated technology has been some conflicting use of commercial satellites. This has become an issue of U.S. Constitutional concern that has not been argued in the court to a constitutional level of liability. Conditionally these problems can be mentally, physically, financially, and even fatally harmful which has been stated as an Endless Loop Crisis. Some would say amendments to the U.S. Constitution are social-economic concerns, but as mass murders increased which may include suicide, a distinct social-technology problem (contrary to health issues) is vitally apparent.

The social-technology mental issues of concern consist of a conflict with mental health which has become an Endless Loop Crisis. This crisis totally looks like some people have lost all "conscious thinking" to the forces of unlawful satellite use, or some other form of un-humanizing technology. These conditions of illegal technology and social behavior exist with a level of unlawful Constitutional liability.

The concept of" simple, and complex", levels of technology have recently consisted of complex issues. These issues have occasionally been part of some monopolized businesses like AT&T, GTE, General Electric (c/o NBC), Raytheon, Eastman Chemicals, Monsanto, and a few others or their subsidiaries. Truly Ameritech with William Daly (c/o AT&T) was one the worse! Even U.S. government agencies like the "monopolized control" of some NASA, NOAA, or U.S. Defense restricted products then became a concern of responsible discipline. Between 1920 and 1945 these issues where part of studies by Robert

Goddard (c/o orbital rockets), and Arthur Clark (c/o satellites) combining the role of rockets, and various satellite technology.

Understanding wireless communication, satellites, and the internet issues of technology we now find Domestic Tranquility in America and somewhat internationally have become good, bad, and conditionally conflicting. This was recognized and partly argued in various violent disturbances consisting of "domestic murder, mass murders, and occasionally with suicide". Circumstantial non-physical and physical conditions of evidence could be considered in the violent 1999 attacks of Columbine, the 1995 Oklahoma federal building bombing, and in 2012 with the Sandy Hook elementary school shooting. Also this included the 2007 Virginia Tech massacre, and massive domestic murder suicide cases in a vast amount of American regions.

Observing various human made tragedies we must remember most good, and bad commercial satellite use is not visible to the human eye. This visibility issue of information transition is conducted with a high capacity of inadmissible activity throughout the American airspace which becomes totally confusing to a vast amount of citizens, or victims. In 1945 Arthur Clark wrote about satellites, and then in 1946 the Rand Corporation wrote about how some satellite activity could be similar to the explosion of the "atom bomb". Then during the 1970s & 80s the Open Skies Policy (c/o the FCC) was considered with the conclusion that public interest with access to commercial satellites would be best served with affording logical opportunities to qualified (contrary to lawful) applicants. Therefore understanding technology and satellites with different results, and studies various people loss mental control, and became defendants of severely bad acts of crime on a lower level of destruction that could not be described easily.

The condition of non-physical evidence (c/o commercial satellites) is strongly possible for what made so many people commit such horrible acts of violence. Rupert Murdoch contrary to any satellite crimes or negligence has been very active in projects considered as "Sky A" & "Sky B" which is part of the Open Skies Policy within the society of the United States and government. Also the Obtaining of Information Illegally (c/o cell phone hacking scandals) that was a relevant law case with Rupert Murdoch's "News of the World" London newspaper publication during 2011 consisted of concerns "which in other American law cases" is rarely prosecuted. The understanding of these issues have, possibly provoked violence or financial disasters which the American system of government has a complex problem in solving.

The U.S. Constitution's legal discipline of prosperity and more so domestic tranquility is conflicting if electronic frequency technology laws are not established, and or enforced. This is part of businesses, organizations, government, and other people pursuing law violations that effect innocent people, or the rights of others destructively when inadmissible central laws of technology are not considered. Then this becomes the issue within wireless communications consisting of technology details that must be more secure. This severely applies to Humans VS the various activity of machinery, computers, satellites, or chemicals. These are technological products that were manufactured to exceed any logical capacity of any human or man to compete against certain man made technology. Some would say this is just like man lifting the heaviest rock in the world, or to swim through an active volcano.

The "News of the World" legal arguments, is conditionally different from companies like AT&T, General Electric, and Raytheon in the awareness that these corporate businesses have aggressive, and diversified products, and or various services. AT&T with their competitor Verizon Communication Inc has created a wireless network that resourcefully exceeds the American system of communication frequencies between 1919 to the 1980s. General Electric, Westinghouse, Radio Corporation of America (RCA), National Broadcasting Corporation (NBC), and what has become the U.S. Department of Defense today has been some of the more complex or aggressive corporate, and government concerns for individuals to argue against in the courts. This is understood through their long term existence, the protection of products, and their level of personal or corporate cash liquidity.

Understanding radio communication frequencies go back to World War I upon which the U.S. government became the "War Department controlling monopoly for this technology", this was done to manage wartime efforts. Also these issues became conditional evidence to certain levels of "national security". Upon comparing World War I, and now Americas war in Iraq and Afghanistan (c/o 2001) with wireless communications, and satellite technology worldwide, certain monopolies with dictatorships, and even terrorist groups have established conflicting control. These products are, and have been a weakness to America against terrorist groups especially when they use some, but not all of the same technology. These factual issues can hinder the United States government, and its people (c/o small and some large businesses) if we as Americans are not careful.

Some issues and problems go along the subject line; that if a group of people would attack the United States on 9-11-2001, they would also violate important U.S. Anti-Trust laws. Observing the oil and gas industry in America more people from the Middle East have gain majority ownership in numerous gas stations at monopolizing rates. This has occurred between the years of 1995 and 2010 to the extent of some of these gas stations being "family or owned by one person" consisting of resources that some are "unlawfully controlled by location ownership legal issues". This is due to the fact that they are located right across the street from each other. Understanding this even a street corner monopoly with Standard Oil Company gas stations along with other major oil companies was outlawed in the early 1920s. Therefore this seems like America has suffered from international investments that lead to international terrorism with little concern about U.S. Anti-Trust laws that affected other rich or expanding business controlled owners.

The recent issues since 1990 of international investments and international terrorism have been an increasing threat with wireless communication, satellite technology, and other dangerous or hazardous issues. One factor is that journalist traveling throughout the world with other people, and solders from America have been stationed in the Middle East, and other places upon which news of technology spreads. Also as more foreign students from diversified countries attend college in the United States, they most times acquire a resource of technology. This technology is offered to them, and occasionally it conditionally is taken home to unstable regions of the world. The format of this is factual about the expanded concern to sale or support the use of new and advanced technology like sophisticated cell phones, and laptop computer activity, which includes their workable networks. Then as ambitious people with lawful or unlawful ideas certain technology and various problems are exposed in most good, bad, or conflicting international ways.

As additional issues are considered the concept of wireless communication then includes how individuals and business are supported by anti-trust laws, and the U.S. Constitution. These are the factors of how the best technology within the United States which goes back to the (U.S.) War Department in the 1930s with times of concern, tried to appropriate the best or winning solutions for the American society. Even though these were World War times of "conflict" business, government, and technology had their different concerns of restrictions, and the (U.S.) War Department without "the Congress" most times won! Therefore we observe justice in the courts, and society as not just winning, but also providing a valid level of compensation, and or a lawful way of living that is appropriated through Constitutional liability.

The stability within recent issues of liability throughout the American society has lately been troublesome by people due to the economy, and the lack of moral and lawful decision making. This conditionally includes the loss of traditional business startups like in Architecture and Engineering firms, Accounting firms, and Real Estate companies. These business concerns have been affected by cities filing for bankruptcy or those whom are real close to problems of economic insolvency. These few professions are not normally monopolies, or the highest earning businesses in society, but they play a big role. This is part of the continued development of America's resource of social, and infrastructure concerns with local and regional government advancements.

The concept of appropriated support for logical business, employment, and the support of young professionals is vital for a city's infrastructure, business values, and other professional and social concerns. Upon even observing engineering, law, accounting, and other professions the U.S. economy has also been a pivotal factor with the slowdown of upgrading the infrastructure, and even the recent 2013 U.S. government shutdown. The recent government shutdown is an argument over the debt ceiling, the Affordable Care Act, and then a lack of tax revenue which is part of the ailing U.S. economy. Then as it applies to the housing market that has been part of a recession during the first 2 decades of 2000 U.S. Constitutional law issues are a low level concern except with consideration of the Affordable "Health" Care Act.

Understanding the U.S. economy in the 2nd decade of 2000, and certain U.S. Constitutional law concerns consisting of wireless communication, and satellite technology are vitally important, but with fractional issues that apply. Two of the major issues of commercial satellite use is the prediction of weather, and air-traffic control. Even as aircrafts with radar, and weather forecast have vital conditions to incorporate into their resource of social conditions, this has been a vital American foundation for the people, and industry. These are factors of not just warning people about deadly storms, but also for airports to coordinate air-traffic communications for safe departures, and arrivals.

Within the changing times in America certain commercial satellite activity has now become useful to various companies like Walmart connecting some 3,000 retail stores. Also during the 1st decade of 2000 most all cable television programming is part of commercial satellite transmissions with digital technology upon which all televisions in the United States had to be reprogrammed. This was an order from the Federal Communication Commission, upon which all televisions had to be cable ready, or have a converter box. Therefore as these massive industries endure changes the format of an economic expansion is relevant, but this does not reconstruct the overall American economic level of security.

A factual concern of cable television and some monopolizing utilities have slightly had tuff economic times due to various unstable markets. The concept of other industries like the housing market with massive foreclosures, have kept these markets in stalemate. This is factored upon how an enormous amount of people have been held back from providing stable payments to cable television companies, and on occasions other utility obligations. Observing this is not directly important to the Constitution of the United States or sometimes the individual state constitution, this is a consideration of facts occasionally with vital service commitments. Conditionally this becomes an issue upon which the laws of the state and federal Constitution must be evaluated when problems need to be solved.

Understanding the difference, of AT&T Corporation, Verizon Communications, Comcast, and others is that they have become productive with the government in taxing their services, and products. The format of taxes by AT&T have been more creative along with government disciplines, but with satellite crimes most all taxable values have been dissolved, or disrupted. Then with more than 100 million customers paying bills with sales taxes the equation in government for this one business or industry is minimal. Therefore as American people pay taxes on these services, and then Americans find themselves in disastrous events, the concept of taxable revenue is loss without invested value for long term stability.

The format of telecommunication and other technological services which provide taxable revenue to government is part of Constitutional liability. This has become a liability that America has lost track of with too many other issues that have been part of complacent government enforcement. These factors are observed as a vitally small fraction of the corporate bailouts during the 1st decade of 2000. Then even though the housing market was a big part, certain unlawful technology played a critical role in the economic level of insecurity to maintain stability. Understanding this, massive amounts of American households loss, and this caused a dysfunctional business, and tax revenue outcome.

CHAPTER FOURTEEN

The Liability Of Monopolies, Business, & The Infrastructure

An American Study Of Business & Monopolies

The Liability Of Monopolies, Business, & The Infrastructure

The resource of most all monopoly businesses in America, usually hold a high standard of liability. This is a factor that sometimes goes along with good customer service, government legislature, and business commitment values of being productive without destructive delays. Contrary to good customer service and dependable liabilities all resources of monopolies are not perfect, but the stronger their cash liquidity is the more they can be efficient, and liable. This is recognized between some private or publicly owned water companies, and wastewater treatment business operation facilities which are government owned with occasional conflicting cash liquidity. Then also too much politics between government and professionalism can cause even more unprofessional problems of inefficiency as a monopolized utility.

The concept of liability is sometimes indifferent from corporate businesses making mistakes consisting of bad accidents like with railroad, coal mining, pharmaceutical companies, and oil company issues. These issues and accidents cause harm to employees, and or occasionally local citizens. Then this level of inefficient liability usually cost the business large amounts of money, and public opinions of hardship.

Certain companies like Commonwealth Edison (Com Ed), Consolidated Edison (Con Ed), Arizona Public Service Co, Northern Indiana Public Service Co, California Edison, and Pacific Gas & Electric which includes others, all have suffered some liability issues. Now compare these few electric utility companies with the general public's access to the internet with various conditions of insecurity which has caused a diversion with future business. This will outline different liability problems with immature or devilish people using the internet to provoke murder or suicide which has become a major problem. Therefore when some public utility accidents, various commercial satellite activity, or internet access activity causes harm to citizens, this gives the American society and system of government issues they must observe and correct.

The concentration of problems that monopolizing the internet and satellite communication can cause has been tremendous. As this occurs the transfer of agreed services rarely occur without regulation, and this is due to the effort of a monopolized systems with limited choices. Understanding a public utility company's resource of monopolizing effort, various internet technology businesses as a growing concern have been important within business matters that must be reestablished.

The concept of Facebook, Twitter, and a few others will work to maintain profitable business over regulation in most good or bad ways. These are the decisions of legislative concern that must be observed for government intervention! This capacity of concern is a destructive issue of trial and error for the American society of all people. Then this becomes the fact of a young person not being mature to understand the good, and bad of how the American society truly works apart from being victimized by what is lawfully right in a normal U.S. lifestyle with laws.

Liabilities now even consist of good, and bad internet issues of conflict. Besides enormous information that is available some applications may hold back progress or sometimes destroy people in several ways. This has been observed with the Affordable Care Act (Obamacare) which has good, and bad concerns, but has recently been complex for most normal American citizens. These are citizens that have an understanding to use the internet to do their business, but all Americans don't have internet access or sometimes even consistent telephone services. With the internet these have been issues of a defect within liability when vast amounts of people totally depend on computer data base operations. Then even defamation with other harmful network crimes or negligence becomes the Constitutional Amendment issues that have occasionally spun out of control.

Negligence with closely held monopolies is an issue that has been observed with large and small public and or private businesses alike. During the 1990s, and the 1st decade of 2000 a diverse amount of explosive accidents with damage have been some of the worse with liable negligence in America's recent times. A 2005 Texas City, Texas BP/Amoco explosion was the worse since 1947. Contrary to this BP refinery that use to be owned by Amoco Oil Corporation, another BP explosion in the Gulf of Mexico occurred in 2010. Understanding the monopolized potential of this company a vast amount of issues, were vital to be corrected for future safety, and numerous valued business resources.

Observing the level of negligence along with other chemical plants which suffered tremendous explosions, equipment damages, and injuries with fatalities certain safety disciplines have a reconstructive need. Some of these safety precautions were quite simple, but others within the overall operations required attention and sometimes professional and government insight which became vital. This became an issue with other concerns of where, educated people became complacent, and refuse to give appropriate training to others with logical skills to do the job.

Considering complex accidents, other major liability issues with fatalities during the 1990s have been slightly corrected. This included northern Indiana's Bata Steel Corporation's 1996 massive explosion from the burning extraction of a gas pipe. The explosive force destroyed parts of the steel plant similar to other explosions throughout the United States which has become a tremendous set back. The Bata Steel Corporation explosion killed 3 contract workers, and injured numerous others with the manufacturing facility severely damaged before repairs started.

Contrary to monopolies the liability cost before, and after certain tragedies is conflicting and critical. This includes the issued duties of the United States Department of Labor which has provided some good and bad duties on the valued subjects of industry and manufacturing liability safety standards. Throughout various parts of the United States such as in Danvers, Massachusetts (2006) a chemical plant exploded, and the facility was leveled clear to the ground. No one was injured in Danvers. Then another chemical textile plant in Morganton, North Carolina suffered an explosion with a chemical fire, and at least 16 employees injured. This Synthron Incorporated chemical plant in North Carolina with its headquarters in Paris, France was completely destroyed in Morganton. Also a chemical plant in Kansas City, Missouri (2006) had a "Propane tank explosion" that ignited with other chemical tanks with enormous flames, and fire, but no one was injured. Therefore 2006 and 2007 seem to very bad years of liability for manufacturing, negligence, and conflicting crime.

As more problems occurred, in Milwaukee, Wisconsin (2006) the Falk Corporation suffered an explosion that killed 3 employed people, and injured 46 other people working at the plant. This Milwaukee, Falk Corporation facility was caused by a "Propane" tank problem during their manufacturing process of metal gears, and other steel mechanical parts. Each and every one of these plant explosions caused damages, and the normal capacity of production, and business was delayed, and or shutdown. This means their business liability especially with chemical processes (c/o propane) affected the earnings of money for the products that they make, and sale. Upon this suffering within economic financial losses to the businesses, employees, and others including government the necessity of liability will have to improve throughout most American industries from overall stability.

Observing these former issues of monopoly, and or closely monopolizing market controlling business issues the larger they are, the more damage they can cause. These damages occur to the environment with the occasional loss of life, and then they have to argue law cases which sometimes determines who is liable through a court proceeding for the disaster. These corporate businesses like the BP/Amoco, and Exxon Corporation with conflicting incidents have endured good income with valued products, but also they have suffered an array of tremendous accidents or negligence. The BP/Amoco explosion killed 14 workers, and injured at least 100 others in 2005. Then during 2010 the BP Gulf of Mexico accident consisted of 11 oil rig workers killed, and 12 others injured. This Gulf of Mexico accident with large quantities of gushing oil into the waterways, and on the seashores of Louisiana was an extreme problem. Therefore these tragic liability issues are a vital economic concern to all involved.

The Exxon Corporation (during 1989, and 1990) was factored with a huge liability and tragic accident, and condition of negligence when the Exxon Valdez oil tanker spilled 11 million gallons of oil into the Gulf of Alaska coastal waters. This environmental disaster and accident perpetuated the killing of birds, and certain fish wildlife. During this accident it also caused heavy concentrations of severely oil contaminated sea waters. The Exxon Corporation spent tens of millions of dollars on "cleanup", and the rescue or survival of sea life animals was somewhat intense. Therefore years later during the early to mid-1990s they needed additional money, and helpful asset liquidity within business.

A concept of this Exxon accident was occasionally part of the restructuring help, and logical discipline of some mergers, and certain corporate work requirements. It is important to observe, and remember that the Exxon Corporation understood the serious nature of the Alaska oil spill disaster from the start. Then by taking control of the problem at the start in all phases, 10 to 15 years later the Exxon Oil Corporations earnings have increased beneficially to the top of the corporate business list. This was established "financially' with likes & dislikes (c/o the CEO and earnings), but as a very productive business operation. Understanding logical business values this is where the (Exxon Corp & Mobil Corp) ExxonMobil Corporation was a merger of possible good with productive and logical business creation factors.

Some of these issues are different from the Buffalo Creek dam collapse & flood of West Virginia in 1972 which has given America a forward and backwards issue of real safety, and design requirements. This is a vital concern apart from effective engineering designs, and the earths many types of foundations. Even as American engineers and construction workers learned and sacrificed a lot within building the Hoover Dam, decades later disciplines of technology, safely responsibilities with regulations were established. These issues became a vital part of hopefully better engineering and construction management duties of a dams overall project regulation and professional responsibilities.

Understanding this, the West Virginia accident also consisted of contractors working for the community whom loss 125 citizens in this disastrous "Dam" event. These become vital industry and government needs for upgraded standards which continued to be a vital and logical issue. This also includes numerous railroad derailments which consisted of occasional chemical spills. Upon this observation making the concept of safety as a job one has become labor issues of suffering with evaluations. These liable conditions even included a massive explosion in San Bruno, California during 2010 which affected a massive amount people, and assets. This explosion was caused by Pacific Gas & Electric which destroyed numerous houses, and caused an a enormous amount of neighborhood infrastructure damages.

Therefore some monopolized utility issues can cause massive disasters which during the 1990s thru 2000 have somewhat been out of control.

Various publicly owned corporate business issues with market or product controlling activity have levels of diversified professional disciplines with liability. This is slightly different from corporate or government public utilities which are slightly similar at the level of some monopolies. Food and pharmaceutical business operations have changed from the traditional farm market trading post production or traveling medicine salesman to a more complex system. This advanced system, consist of computerized industrial processes, and business networks with massive amounts of sale representatives. Then this means more machinery, more chemicals, more packaging with distribution, and even more professional issues of management. Therefore regional public utility monopolies, or the medicine monopolized sale of products must be a bit more committed to safety, and customer satisfaction. This usually exist with public utility companies providing electricity, gas, and water having lately become the better or more financially secure part of providing various utility services.

Most food and pharmaceutical companies in America consist of products with complex or logical ingredients that company's and corporations spend time researching, and developing. This is the format of business disciplines within conditional and effective manufacturing processes. These businesses usually consist of a strong concept of corporate liquidity to value the cost of these important procedures, discoveries, and sale's that usually improve. Some of the American pharmaceutical companies of today with disciplines of research consist of Pfizer Inc., Merck & Company, Eli Lilly & Company, Abbott Laboratories, Johnson & Johnson Inc, Baxter International, and others that have past and future potential. Understanding progress these consolidated businesses with some universities doing research on products that make advancements for the American general public, are then reviewed by the U.S. Food and Drug Administration.

Certain United States government procedures also consist of the Food and Drug Administration (FDA) conducting additional research with clinical and testimonial evidence in hearings. This is the approval procedures for safely recommended new medicines, and the review of other products that may be questionable within liability. Observing this internal medicine approval process, these levels of evaluation give the U.S. government's approval within the safety, and effectiveness of medicine, and various resources of disciplined medical procedures. Understanding this concern, the FDA was established to enforce the Food, Drug, and Cosmetic Act which has a concern for any products that could have harmful effects, and how they are offered to citizen / patients of the American general public. These liability concerns to protect the health of American citizens become an issue for the many products that various companies make as food, drugs, and or cosmetics.

The American market's for food products over the last 50 to 100 years has went through many different changes. A few of the largest American food company's (c/o also beverage companies) are Kraft Foods, ConAgra Foods, Kroger, Monsanto, Coca Cola, PepsiCo, Kellogg Company, and Tyson Foods. Considering this understanding, some of the most productively expanding businesses and corporations consist of cash liquidity values, and issues that must be pursued with careful evaluation. For hundreds of years Americans have found, and created medicine products that help solve medical problems, and food to feed the people so that they can live with good rates of nutrition, and therefore valid conditions of liability were established.

Over the years products have went through the conditional format of lawful elimination. This becomes the modification process of food and pharmaceutical items that hopefully don't make people severely sick, and or with additional illness conditions. The moderation, and procedures of shipping, content of food ingredients, and now the relevant good health of farm raised animals are consistent with all parts of this step by step market, and liability process. Understanding this variation of commodities is the life line of American food, beverages, and the medical industry. This includes all business values of logical "cost and earning" factors to its many consumers within customers, and the company.

Within the "American Markets of Pharmaceutical" products, a vast amount of over-the-counter drugs, and pharmaceutical prescribed drug products have had to endure the changing times of America. Just like food companies, the pharmaceutical companies have had to bring in good products, and then take out certain bad products which may be part of a lawsuit, or a United States major health concern. This evaluation process is a liability issue of argumentative conditions by the company that develops, and manufactures the best products possible, and what health or food conditions it will improve. This is also associated with the administrated duties of the FDA for the regulated purity of food, the effectiveness of medicines, and various therapeutic devises.

It is important in this format to the FDA that these products have truthfulness within labels, and safety with the honesty of packaging. Understanding packaging, and distribution of medicines from various pharmaceutical companies during 2007 they provided doctor's offices with more than 240,000,350 samples. These samples of medicine held a value of more than $3.26 billion dollars to market their products. Then these are usually considered their best products upon which they sale large volumes of medicine to the medical industry throughout the vast amount of communities in America. Therefore there is a level of confidence that "most, but not all" of these medical products are workable with high rates of liability which means periodic reviews become important.

Observing doctors, and patents that endure various good, and occasionally bad medical products that don't perform well, this can cause a severe effect to liabilities, professional standards, various people, and certain values of the market. Contrary to medicine, throughout the American food supply of products this also becomes a problem when food products are not cared for properly "similar to medicine" with various process procedures. It is relevant to say, and understand that various exquisite restaurants, and grocery stores that can provide excellent food products, and services for preparing meals can be affected by this problem if they are not careful. Even drug stores with a small or large volume of store locations, and customers must maintain a format of liability including the resource of choosing some non-prescription medication items that are the best logical products. Contrary to this market issue, this becomes a matter of business owners and professionals that choose the best or most logical products they can offer.

This format of products also consist of the short term, or long term complaints from customers that must be evaluated. Considering large retail drug stores like Walgreen's Co., Osco Drug's, CVS

Caremark Corp and grocery stores like Safeway similar to restaurants like McDonald's, Burger King, Red Lobster and a few others, they have liability, and customer satisfaction managing disciplines that distinctively apply. These corporate businesses stress these values that go along the resource of their established business plan for employees. Sometimes this cost within the best items is part of a market discipline within managing, and potential earnings with the volume of effective or satisfied customers to keep a productive establishment as a valued business resource.

The insurance industry concerning numerous, liabilities and American disasters have consisted of a strong combination of issues in various regions. These are regions of America which during the 1990s, and the 1st decade of 2000 have cost insurance companies tremendous amounts of money. This was the effect of man-made and nature forced disasters that sometimes the American society of people, and professionals could have been better prepared for with the infrastructure and issues of contingent emergency problems. With this understanding the concept of numerous professional values like engineering and construction that upgrades the infrastructure, and together with government officials making the best and most productive decisions becomes a vital concern.

Considering our American society within the years of the late 1990s, and the first decade of 2000 the American people witnessed, and suffered with their American ownership of managed assets being destroyed by the force of nature, and other conflicting events of concern. The forceful nature considering events such as hurricanes, mudslides, forest wildfires, a few earthquakes in certain regions, and a vast amount of storm water flooded regions has stun various American people, and their livable standards. This has also made asset protection problems complex. These issues are a vital concern within government, and various markets similar to insurance, and even the logic of professional engineering. Therefore these become some of the people's value within business, and society whom can provide workable solutions during the 2000 decade, and future with logical decisions usually sustained through government.

Another complex problem includes a normal capacity of tornados that have factored, and applied unlivable conditions to various parts of America. These regions within being a "State and or Federal

Declared Disaster" which consisted of severely damaged assets of lawful property had vital personal and insured issues of cost, and then people loss or had to restructure. Understanding this process it clearly becomes important that certain "extensive" conditions of property value must be adjusted. The items of value (c/o some insured) would include vehicles, houses, or other non-replaceable items, and or personal documented assets.

Closely understanding and observing the insurance companies of America, one of the worse financial conditions of damage that was caused to a region was the Southern Central Gulf States disaster from the 2005 Hurricane Katrina that destroyed parts of Mississippi, and a vast amount of New Orleans, Louisiana. Although the United States government is committed to helping the Gulf States, and more so the recovery of New Orleans with different services, and money a vast amount of insurance company officials have been slightly puzzled with cost, and procedures. These insurance company official's, and lawyers are looking and debating large policy damage issues that have effected residential homes, commercial facilities, and business districts that included heavily damaged assets. This process is slightly different because more lawyers are involved considering there is more than the normal amount of annual processing clams involved with some court proceedings.

These Gulf States regional concerns, and business issues between different insurance companies, with a vast amount of good, and bad government opinions have conflicting subjects which will require massive work. Within the general public, and the (state & federal) government this problem will require the determination of people, and business including government to closely work together. This massive work effort is due to these loads of tremendous damage. The tremendous factors of damage also consist of workable cost, more up-graded infrastructure asset cost, and some overtime non-factored bonuses within cost. Hopefully everything within these sacrifices will be done right, and therefore the prevention within infrastructures will be improved! It also becomes important to remember that within the Gulf States of America including Texas, Mississippi, Florida, and Louisiana (c/o New Orleans), various business markets have suffered some of these severe cost factors, and damage's.

Besides the large markets of fish, shrimp, and lobsters in these markets, there was a considerable amount of off-shore oil drilling rigs that were damaged during hurricane Katrina. This factored a slow-down in the oil business production activity in the Gulf of Mexico throughout this American region, but the oil industry sometimes has a way of putting themselves back in production. Therefore the Gulf of Mexico within these international waters of the United States is part of some people's place of work that have been damaged, including a vast amount of these people's homes that they reside in outside of work. This even forced a vast amount of people to leave that Gulf States region to truly have a responsible life.

Homes, schools, hospitals, church's businesses, and government offices were damaged in hurricane Katrina. This was factual considering the vast amounts of assets that were damaged during this 2005 hurricane which included the factual problem within the partly insured recovery. The U.S. President George Bush declared the region a Disaster Area with an appropriate state of Emergency for assisting the people that tried to ride the storm out at home. Then the observed conditions of those regional areas became worse for those people in 9th Ward homes which included wiped out utilities, and severe infrastructure damage. Assessments of "damage" is, and became a very important fact about the cleanup from a hurricane, and or more so the flooding. This assessment process most times includes the factors within insurance compensation payments, and most all level of government operating cost that provides an equation to solve factual problems with emergency solutions.

These problems of a catastrophic capacity consist of various dangerous levels of contamination that were submerged in the flood waters consisting of things such as oil, paint, and other poisonous contaminates. Some problems would also include the regional dogs, cats, rates, poisonous snakes, reptile alligators, and other habitants. Observing these factors, it was very important that young children must be severely guided, and closely supervised by their parents or other's during this disaster. Then this was included in the process of cleaning which included an effect of survival with asset recovery disciplines. Some elderly people truly had a hard time surviving without productive young people helping for their surviving concerns. In addition within this hurricane (Katrina) during 2005 it had a storm after mass which consisted of vast amounts of dead people, and animal body remains that were found compounded in the devastating flood waters. This sustained problem that existed for weeks increased the levels of contaminated water that was tremendous until cleanup, upon which at the same time young and more so older people were accounted for as deceased, or living.

Upon this catastrophic disaster, and concern over 1,500 people died in the flood waters. A vast amount of animals (dead or alive) were removed from that contaminated water, and subdued wet lands. This also included various household and commercial chemical products that modified this diversified process of massive insurance clams, and cleanup with many different types of illnesses. In addition the consolidated factors of future evaluations, is a duty and priority that will have to be governed. This also includes being managed by various involved professionals with business priorities, and the concern of citizens.

Observing this disaster even the concern of the local police, and fire department officials had to stabilize people stealing from different retail stores to get what they needed, and sometimes wanted. Considering this issue, it offered additional problems, and losses (c/o some insured) that were hard, and complex to avoid. This therefore was observed, and considered as a total restriction of life with non-livable standards from the disaster that had occurred. Observing the evaluation of this massive problem in America, this is the considered fact of a consolidated problem to be the total concept within a disaster.

Another factor within this terrible hurricane Katrina disaster also caused suffering which was a loss of government assets, and most logical communication systems. During most storms of this capacity occasionally telephone cables are "damaged", and this destroys that operating system, and the format of people making contact and talking to other people on telephones. Considering this, most factors within government communication, and various official duties included the loss of certain New Orleans police department officials, and most social values becoming a governed condition of worrisome factors.

In addition to police, and fire department officials not able to maintain complete order, different levels of government still had emergency step by step duties. This hurricane Katrina caused problems to all electrical power which had been blacked out with no time consideration of when the public utilities would be restored. Considering this problem of working in the dark of the night to rescue stranded people, most efforts became complex and somewhat dangerous for everyone in New Orleans.

This array of problems following the hurricane also includes the duties within what it takes for people to be rushed to the nearest hospitals of appropriate operating capacity to have safe, and responsible health care matters diagnosed, and treated. These professional service issues are relevant in certain hospital facilities that survived various aspects of the flooding, storm, and hurricane's wind force. It's no doubt that this was one of the worse "government, and engineering" disasters of our American society. These were the times of today "due to obsolete' storm water retention levees that failed, and caused trauma. Although "Mother Nature" is not an easy one to control, this therefore consisted of the consideration that the American society (c/o New Orleans) could have done better to prevent, and be prepared for this issue. This then severely includes the disaster within insurance business repercussion values that was severe to adjust.

The hospitals and other businesses also consist of insurance concerns that appropriate their operating capacity of liability. Observing the format of liabilities that are required to work with the local, counties, states, and even various federal government officials became relevant with professional disciplines. Observing this, these people with duties were subjected to the most extreme conditions of surviving a storm in America. Also these conditions consisted of providing security, and efficient control to guide stranded citizens out of flooded areas to safer places.

The discipline and factor of ethics consisting of U.S. Anti-Trust laws of equality including minority contractor issues (c/o some non-bid contracts) were considered. This was observed to coordinate any local contractors that could be helpful between business and government to restructure this massive city concern. Also these factored issues within the format that professional government contractors that were needed, and considered after "law, and order" was reestablished the format of Americans working together became relevant.

Observing these factors of logic within hurricane Katrina this means the complex amount of cost that remained, and with workable duties would be completely understood. This became important with other concerns of a well-developed society upon which this disaster had to be completely evaluated. Considering this financial, and contractual business issue it included certain Architecture, Engineering, and Construction contractors from Louisiana (c/o New Orleans), and other different parts of America. A valid concern is that they would have to comply with the U.S. individual states, and federal Constitutional laws although special amendments were applied. This was vital to get hospitals, paramedics, police, and fire department officials back in operating order. Therefore mandates to restore the "New Orleans Metropolitan Area" was set on an agenda, but it also was an agenda with conditional government legislative amendments. Then this became a fact that would take years, and even decades for certain levels of a full recovery.

When an individual as well as insurance company official's looked, and reviewed the cost of various business or survival concerns certain observation became important. These were issues similar to people subjected to medical procedures of a hospital, and how it consist the expenses of a critical medical operation. A normal medical operation of internal medicine procedures will consist of an hour or more of professional liabilities (diverting light, water, oxygen fixtures, and other equipment on and off) with special nurse assistance procedures, and different medications. Sometimes these are multiple operations at one time. Also this includes a vast amount of special tools, and materials that the professional medical surgeon requires for a successful surgery in an operating room environment.

Hospital disciplines, just like other businesses, or tools, and the ways within conducting professional procedures must be done right. Observing this professional procedure is part of making this the consideration of partial duties of most all professional disciplines of liability workable. Then as Americans, within business markets with certain liability's observe these people as they are (and must be) careful to provide professional, and occupational standards of astute procedures. Therefore these concerned factors which become the regular standard of good, and bad lawful professional decisions most times they find efficiency.

Another problem and debated concern was the vast amount of inventory that was damaged during this (2005) hurricane Katrina that included cars, and trucks that were located at a vast amount of automobile dealerships. This conditional concern includes massive amounts of vehicles that were owned by the metropolitan issues of government, businesses, and the people of New Orleans. Then the city, town, and state constituents found a command cause of asset concerns. Within this combination of vehicles with asset claims, there was hundreds of thousands of vehicles destroyed, or damaged severely, and this factor, and cost had many good, and bad insured variations.

Only a certain amount of automobile dealerships, and other businesses restructured before most individual citizen's and some smaller businesses. This was a vital business diversion apart from those businesspeople, and citizens that relocated or closed a business after the disasters of hurricane Katrina with discretionary restructuring. These were the facts of some business owners that refused all odds to not take a complete loss, and not leave New Orleans. Another factor includes their small, or large capacity of inventory that could not be saved, and this compiled factual losses. Some things within products or inventory are insured, and some items and things are not which some people were prepared for. As a factual cost was vital to consolidate the awareness to continue the balance of most all business bookkeeping in the American Gulf States consisted of present, and future business concerns of determination.

Contrary to the insurance business factor within conducting the duties of certain business operations this recovery process was becoming complex considering how the government with public, private businesses had to work together. This was observed when the levees of the City of New Orleans collapsed, and the flood water capacities became rational. Therefore the fact that the levees around New Orleans were built in the mid to late 1960s with the Flood Control Act of 1965 it outlined that regular inspections were mandatory. Upon this observation this is where various issues of government became complacent.

These levees where built as government assets to protect the citizens, and society which means the maintenance with vital upgrades of this floodwall system was ignored. This lack of governed awareness destroyed the safety, assets, and liability of the people. Also the flood waters caused most of these damages, and this means our American society of engineering, and government consisted of severe problems that need fixing. Some or most of the people of Louisiana should hope that Mayor Ray Nagan, and others have learned from this disaster. The actual wind and rain from the hurricane was one factor, but the flood waters from the levee system that collapsed is what caused these human fatal, and property damage issues at various historical rates.

Throughout the United States the many geographical regions of our American industry of insurance companies is part of numerous resources. These insurance companies have commitments to businesses, and numerous households that have been hit with record amounts of damage. Then most all have hopes that claims can be adjusted, and compensated. So, observing various recent historical disasters this has accumulated financial damages to businesses, and the property people own at some of the worse means possible.

Earthquakes are one of the many bad conditions with damages especially in states like California, and its geographical atmosphere. During the late 1990s, and the early 2000s mudslides and forest wildfires became another catastrophic problem in California, and a few other western states. These geographical, social, and financial concerns consisted of some insurance companies, and the people which found these issues to be vitally observant to maintain. Also it has become relevant that government and others like utility companies do productive work to help the prevention of these problems, and or protecting the people's property. Therefore as it applies to insurance, and personal business matters these problems carried a high rate of damage in certain regions, and various rates on a policy for insurance which become a debatable value along with property taxes.

The logic of making adjustments to manage most concerns of damage are complex values to the effective needs of protection, and possible compensation within the various detailed types of possible regional disasters. These disasters that occurred in California most times consisted of workable liabilities to be reviewed. This is a vital concern, and consideration about the coverage of claims (c/o adjustments) that had to be appropriately understood, factored, and applied with various adjusted claims, and prevention issues with prepared future levels of caution.

Various catastrophic disasters and other obsolete infrastructures of un-formatted resources of land have created a larger format of liability within the different types of insurance commitments. These have been discretionary, or contingent factors such as mudslides with claim's, wildfire claim's, and tornados with claim's. Claims such as these were newly becoming a conflict because the geological settings were changing tremendously with new construction, and how it coordinated the effect upon financial protection to compensate settlements for these damages. Once the forest wildfire would destroy a majority of trees, then the unattended soil was left soft. As this soil continued to accumulate rainwater it caused ground conditions to break apart causing mudslide conditions as another contingent problem becoming a repeated issue of disasters.

The observation concerning geographic, and development conditions within the West Coast Region of the United States was complex for some people. This was due to the fact that sometimes an earthquake is expected, but mudslides, or wildfires near residential areas became the most serious problem based on contingent liabilities. Therefore changing, or upgrading the geological ground components of sub-grade conditions especially in the mountains is considered a challenge to the solemn state of various people's community of living.

The California mudslides became a very complex liability with severe ground conditions of danger for house's, and roads that were built in the mountains. Observing these mudslides from the higher elevations of the mountains, some houses moved from one location "downward" to another due to massive flowing wet mud. This also eliminated, and destroyed certain roads, and the property lots that certain expensive houses were built on. Also some very expensive houses were still under construction that had none, or incomplete insurance coverage as they were destroyed from these geological conditions. Considering these houses in the mountains, certain California, and Arizona debates with professional arguments existed adding conflicting pressure about building so many houses that were taking up space on the mountains.

Another issue was the congested amount of houses that were taking up space on the mountains which some people acknowledged that this disturbs wildlife, and the prevention of natural values. This vital debate consisted of a few other vital professional factors which had to be considered. That was the control of geographic sub-grade conditions which are slightly unpredictable within mud, and rain applicable with the concern of earthquakes. Considering this combination of natural beauty in the mountains, and these occasionally unpredictable disasters, this conflict stricken region of value throughout the West Coast, and it's scientific conditions becomes complex to predict. Then contrary to certain issues some geological problems could have been observed "preventively".

Considering the liabilities within American business markets with certain geological and engineering studies of research, these evaluation issues become important to consolidate predictions of financial claims, and policy issues of insurance. This becomes the format of business that Scientific Professional's pursue as a format of business procedures, and that is consistent with most applicable insurance, engineering, and even construction business considerations of effective liabilities. Then these factors of general living standards become important evaluated estimates, and predictions. Therefore a good professional observes the lowest level, to the highest level of contingent liability problems possible, but the lower the contingent risk is, the better things are considered.

Upon understanding the differences of contingencies in our American society of business, these are financial, occupational, and professional management issues. This is observed with duties that apply to everything that could happen unexpectedly. Also the issued format of planning, and sacrifices is a vital factor for all people that work to achieve a formal good life. Therefore within managing a home, business, organization, or even a government office with all lawful liabilities, and contingent factors this is how we overcome most problems with the best professional solutions possible.

Most all businesses, industries, and occasionally government consisting of vital market liability duties, and workable effort have manageable concerns to work to observe important procurements. These issues are similar to government or public utility assets that are considered with most contingent liabilities. Considering this they become the asset with procedures that are to be taken serious with most levels of caution. The American automobile industry and the major oil companies of the U.S.A. are logical examples that include oil spills, or vehicle parts that malfunction. Occasionally there is also "pharmaceutical products" that consist of good and bad problems with contingent factors that must be reviewed by law, observed within clinical studies, and understood by industry professionals. Insurance companies, and banking establishments are considered some of the businesses with the highest level of contingent disciplines, and that's why when the American economy is doing good they factor a particular kind of growth, and or stability.

Some companies including banks and insurance agency businesses have suffered failure due a lack of contingent factors with the U.S. economy. This is factual considering some of their disputes to hold on to business which may have been with the different conditions from a failing or unpredictable banking industry. The conditions of these contingent facts in our American society can be the loss of liability, and liquidity that consist of people's day by day survival. This therefore is a factually important subject within most all companies, progress within business conditions of liability, and ethical discipline.

American International Group (AIG), and some other large American insurance companies where effected with contingent financial losses after the September 11, 2001 terrorist attacks. These contingent base losses from AIG amounted to about $500 to $800 million dollars. These, and a few factual subjects such as insuring investment banking activity has lead AIG Inc into the resource of asking the United States government for a financial bailout consideration. This becomes an issue of monopolized insurance mixed with issues of financial liability.

Observing the September 11, 2001 attacks various American insurance businesses loss more than an estimated $50 billion dollars. These are the types of similar losses that were suffered, and or compounded from hurricane Katrina, but the hurricane disaster consisted of more uninsured people, and probably some under-insured, and uninsured businesses. Upon these issues within the American system of government that takes a vast amount of concern for the people, and businesses most all parts of America's general welfare was threatened. This therefore has duties that require vital conditions of effort from government. These have been the factors within the general public which consist of problem's that contingently effect the poorest people, to the wealthiest of people, and most all "residentially started" businesses, and even established corporations.

Index

Printed in the United States
By Bookmasters